ISBN 978-1-5283-3965-0
PIBN 10913633

This book is a reproduction of an important historical work. Forgotten Books uses
state-of-the-art technology to digitally reconstruct the work, preserving the original format
whilst repairing imperfections present in the aged copy. In rare cases, an imperfection in
the original, such as a blemish or missing page, may be replicated in our edition. We do,
however, repair the vast majority of imperfections successfully; any imperfections that
remain are intentionally left to preserve the state of such historical works.

1 MONTH OF
FREE
READING

at

www.ForgottenBooks.com

---◇---

BY
CLIFFORD W. BEERS
AUTHOR OF
"A MIND THAT FOUND ITSELF"

CONTENTS

Quoted from the Revised Fifth Edition of "A Mind That Found Itself," published October, 1921.

the compliments of
Clifford W. Beers

A Mind That Found Itself

By CLIFFORD WHITTINGHAM BEERS

Fifth Edition, revised, containing a separate account of the Mental Hygiene Movement.

NINTH PRINTING OF BOOK
Published in October, 1921, by

LONGMANS, GREEN & CO., 443 Fourth Avenue, New York

368 pp.—8vo.   Price $1.90 net.   By mail, $2.00.

This book has been characterized as "the inspiration of the mental hygiene movement."

"The author's narrative in itself is unique in literature."
—*Review of Reviews.*

"As a story it is far more interesting than most novels. A remarkable book."—*New York Sun.*

"It is a book which once taken up will certainly not be replaced on the book-shelf until every page has been read."
Daily Mail, London, England.

"I read 'A Mind That Found Itself' with profound interest. To me it is a wonderful book. I scarcely remember ever having read anything which stirred me so deeply, or left upon my memory stronger or more vivid impressions."
—*His Eminence, the late Cardinal Gibbons.*

"The interest of the narrative far exceeds that of any novel I have read in a long, long time. I do not believe that any intelligent person, whose attention has ever been called to the subject, will lay down the work willingly after he is once well started in its perusal."—*Thomas R. Lounsbury, late Professor of English Literature, Yale University.*

"I thank you for the new edition of your remarkable book, 'A Mind That Found Itself.' I have been reading it again with a renewed sense of its interest and value. The book is certainly of a most extraordinary quality. A friend of mine sat up nearly all night to read it and said when he brought it back: 'That is more interesting than a novel.'"—*Henry van Dyke.*

The Mental Hygiene Movement

BY

CLIFFORD W. BEERS

AUTHOR OF
"A Mind That Found Itself"

This document contains supplementary material presented in the Revised Fifth Edition of "A Mind That Found Itself" Published in October, 1921

AUTHOR'S NOTE

IN response to a demand for an account of the origin and growth of the work of The National Committee for Mental Hygiene, part of the Revised Fifth Edition of "A Mind That Found Itself," published in October, 1921, is herewith presented in pamphlet form.

C. W. B.

The Mental Hygiene Movement

I

ORIGIN AND GROWTH

IN my autobiography, "A Mind That Found Itself," I make a plea for mental sufferers. But the story of the work that followed in behalf of those sufferers—the story of The National Committee for Mental Hygiene, of State Societies in this country, and of national committees or their equivalent in foreign countries—is now to be told. Though I call this story "The Mental Hygiene Movement," it might not inappropriately be entitled "The Romance of Work." For to me, at least, this work has been a romance, and not wanting in thrills and even in dramatic moments, as one difficulty after another has been overcome.

The story of the work was an integral part of the narrative in earlier editions of "A Mind That Found Itself." My reasons for now making virtually two books of what was formerly one are reflected in the following letter from Professor Wilbur Cross, Editor of *The Yale Review* and Dean of the Graduate School at Yale University.

New Haven, Connecticut,
September 12, 1921.

DEAR MR. BEERS:

Your extraordinary book I have followed with profound interest through its various editions since you showed me a typewritten copy of a preliminary draft more than fifteen years ago. I was absorbed in the story you then told. You may remember that I thought you had the material, which was at that time not wholly in literary form, for an autobiography comparable to De Quincey's ' Confessions.' Through your efforts has since been organized The National Committee for Mental Hygiene, with affiliated State Societies; and agencies similar to the National Committee have been established in foreign countries, and an "International Committee" is in process of formation.

After these accomplishments, it seems most fitting that you should now rearrange the contents of your book by giving the story of your experiences as one continuous narrative while reserving for an appendix all other matters. In the proofs of the revised, 5th Edition of your autobiography, I read without a break the wonderful tale you told me many years ago. You have now produced a strange and thrilling account of your experiences, in such form that the gain for literature is immense. In short, your book is destined to become a classic. Believe me,

Yours most sincerely,
WILBUR L. CROSS.

A leader in the field of psychiatry and mental hygiene, Dr. C. Macfie Campbell, Professor of Psychiatry at Harvard University, who did me the favor of examining the proofs of my revised edition, sent me the following letter:

Cambridge, Mass.,
September 20, 1921.

DEAR MR. BEERS:

I have just read the page proofs of the fifth edition of " A Mind That Found Itself," with the same fascination with which I read the book on its first appearance. Every reader, lay or medical, cannot but be carried away by the rush of the narrative. The psychopathologist may here and there modify the values given by the author and have personal interpretations to suggest, but he finds in the book both a story of absorbing interest and an important clinical document. I admire your courage and talent in having, like Mr. A. C. Benson in "Thy Rod and Thy Staff," transmuted a distressing personal experience into a valuable literary product. What I admire still more is that, while Mr. Benson has produced an essay of great beauty, you have furnished us, not only with a literary ornament, but with a powerful weapon and instrument of social progress.

It is a sharp weapon with which to smite the hydra-headed abuses connected with the treatment of insanity, abuses dependent on mediæval thought, medical ignorance, social indifference, personal greed and insensitiveness, political depravity, financial restrictions. Even more than as a weapon of offence is your book valuable as a peaceful instrument of social improvement.   I do not suppose that, when you were so cheerfully forging this trenchant weapon and thinking of reform, you foresaw how rapid would be the development of the movement represented by The National Committee for Mental Hygiene, of which you were the inspiration.   This movement, which had its origin in a desire to correct abuses, has broadened out into a broad health movement, dealing with those complex functions which mean most to human life.

The National Committee for Mental Hygiene has helped much in relation to the immediate practical problems of mental disorder and defect; it has emphasized the important bearing of these topics on such great social problems as delinquency and dependency of all types; it has consistently aimed at bringing into education principles of prophylactic value, which promise to develop a more robust personality than the traditional education; it would introduce into the management of industrial and economic problems the consideration of factors involving the personality of the individual worker, which in the past have been strangely neglected.

The field of mental hygiene is coextensive with the field of human endeavor; progress cannot be left altogether to the unorganized good-will of the well-meaning, but requires organization of forces and the clear formulation of problems and policies.

I, therefore, consider that in following up the publication of your book by the organization of The National Committee for Mental Hygiene, you have made a social contribution of very great value. Those who have vague ideas on the exact nature and scope of this important movement will find in "A Mind That Found Itself" a tale of intense human interest, and an admirable introduction to some of the practical problems of mental hygiene.

Cordially yours,
C. MACFIE CAMPBELL.

Why I continue to write in an intimate way in this sequel to my first book is indicated in the following letter from Dr. Stephen P. Duggan, Director of The Institute of International Education. Having served for a number of years as a member of the Executive Committee of The National Committee for Mental Hygiene, he speaks from personal knowledge.

NEW YORK CITY,
September 7, 1916.

DEAR MR. BEERS:

As the work done by you in connection with The National Committee for Mental Hygiene is comparable to that done for the insane during the last century by Dorothea Dix and by Pinel in the eighteenth century, you owe it to your readers to tell the story of the organizing of the first "societies for mental hygiene" and of what they have done to focus the attention of the public on the great problem of mental health. This I say advisedly, for even I, a member of the Executive Committee of the National Committee for some time past, did not learn in detail, until recently, of your unique services during the formative period of work.

I know of no better way for you to do this than by quoting some of the many letters sent to you by those who gave moral or financial support, or both, while you were organizing the National Committee and stimulating interest in the mental hygiene movement in general.   These letters, which you kindly let me read when I asked for the intimate story of your pioneer days in mental hygiene work, not only held my attention, but left me with the feeling that everything I could do to further the work should be done.   It seems to me that others privileged to read the opinions mentioned will be similarly affected, with benefit to the cause.

Permit me to say in closing: Do not hesitate to publish the letters in which complimentary references to yourself appear.   One cannot speak well of the work without thinking well of the man who had the moral courage, persistency, and ability to make this important work possible.

Sincerely yours,
STEPHEN P. DUGGAN.

The first step toward organizing The National Committee for Mental Hygiene involved the securing of a publisher for my book—no easy task for an unknown writer, with an unusual subject.   To this end I sought both literary and psychological endorsement.   I surprised the late Professor Lounsbury, in one of whose classes at Yale I had been a not-too-promising student, by appearing before him ten years later with the manuscript of a real story. The letter which he gave me and a direct introduction from Professor William James to Mr. Charles J. Mills, of Longmans, Green & Company, helped me over this first obstacle. Professor Lounsbury's letter read as follows:

New Haven,
March 24, 1907.

Dear Mr. Beers:

I have gone over with great care that portion of your manuscript which you let me have—amounting, as I understand, to about one-half of the whole—and can testify that to me at least the interest of the narrative far exceeds that of any novel which I have read in a long, long time. It strikes me indeed as being something besides a truthful, human document; it is a well-told document, which, one must say regretfully, truthful documents are too often unapt to be. I do not believe, in fact, that any intelligent person, whose attention has been called to the subject, will lay down the work willingly, after he is once well started in its perusal. To its interest I can testify for myself; to its value as an inside account of an insane person's psychology, after the opinion given by such an authority as Professor James, nothing further can properly be said by any one.

Sincerely yours,
Thomas R. Lounsbury.

Professor James's letter of introduction was a formal one. His initial help in advancing the mental hygiene movement is more fully stated in the following excerpt from "The Letters of William James," edited by his son, Henry James, and published in 1920. One of the thrills referred to on a preceding page came to me when I discovered, upon opening the second volume of the "Letters," the following paragraphs:

"The next letter is addressed to an active promoter of reform in the treatment of the insane, the author of 'A Mind That Found Itself.' The Connecticut Society for Mental Hygiene and The National Committee for Mental Hygiene have already performed so great a public service that anyone may now see that in 1907 the time had come to employ such instrumentalities in improving the care of the insane. But when Mr. Beers, just out of an 'asylum' himself, appeared with the manuscript of his own story in his hands, it was not so clear that these agencies were needed, nor yet evident to anyone that he was a person who could bring about their organization.

" James's own opinion of the treatment of the insane is not in the least overstated in the following letter. He recognized the genuineness of Mr. Beers's personal experience and its value for propaganda, and he immeidately helped to get it published. From his first acquaintance with Mr. Beers, he gave time, counsel, and money to further the organization of The National Committee for Mental Hygiene; and he even departed, in its interest, from his fixed policy of 'keeping out of

Committees and Societies.' He lived long enough to know that the movement had begun to gather momentum; and he drew great satisfaction from the knowledge."

CAMBRIDGE, Apr. 21, 1907.

DEAR MR. BEERS:

You ask for my opinion as to the advisability and feasibility of a National Society, such as you propose, for the improvement of conditions among the insane.

I have never ceased to believe that such improvement is one of the most 'crying needs' of civilization; and the functions of such a society seem to me to be well drawn up by you. Your plea for its being founded before your book appears is well grounded, you being an author who naturally would like to cast seed upon ground already prepared for it to germinate practically without delay.

I have to confess to being myself a very impractical man, with no experience whatever in the details, difficulties, etc., of philanthropic or charity organization, so my opinion as to the *feasibility* of your plan is worth nothing, and is undecided. Of course the first consideration is to get your money, the second your Secretary and Trustees. All that *I* wish to bear witness to is the great need of a National Society such as you describe, or failing that, of a society somewhere that might serve as a model in other States.

Nowhere is there massed together as much suffering as in the asylums. Nowhere is there so much sodden routine and fatalistic insensibility in those who have to treat it. Nowhere is an ideal treatment more costly. The officials in charge grow resigned to the conditions under which they have to labor. They cannot plead their cause as an auxiliary organization can plead it for them. Public opinion is too glad to remain ignorant. As mediator between officials, patients and the public conscience, a society such as you sketch is absolutely required and the sooner it gets under way the better.

Sincerely yours,
WILLIAM JAMES.

In securing the endorsement of persons who could speak with authority, it was not only desirable to be vouched for by Professor Lounsbury and by Professor James, who held commanding positions in their respective fields, but most important of all, perhaps, that I should secure the approval of some physician who had made a special study of mental diseases and had first-hand knowledge of the problem of State-care of the insane. I made a step toward securing that approval when I enlisted the interest of Dr. Stewart Paton, who had not served in the State-hospital field, but was a psychiatrist of note. Under date of May 30th, 1907, he wrote as follows:

"It is needless to say that you have my best wishes for success in your undertaking. After reading the manuscript you so kindly sent me, I feel sure intelligent people will listen to your appeal and take an active interest in this work. Surely you will be a public benefactor if you succeed in realizing your ideals."

Dr. Paton told me that Dr. Adolf Meyer, then Director of the Psychiatric Institute of the New York State Hospitals at Ward's Island, New York City, who later became Director of the Phipps Psychiatric Clinic at the Johns Hopkins Hospital, Baltimore, was the one man of all others in his special field whose support should, if possible, be secured. Through the courtesy of Dr. Paton, I was able to submit to Dr. Meyer the page proof of my book and outline my plans. This proved to be a most fortunate occurrence as Dr. Meyer for a long time had wished that some organized auxiliary movement for better care and treatment for the insane and for the prevention of mental disorders might be inaugurated in this country. He and I, therefore, at once began to collaborate.

It is interesting to note that when Dr. Meyer and I first met in September, 1907, he was at a loss to find the word or words that would express not only the idea of amelioration of conditions among the insane, but also the idea of prevention of mental disorders. A few days later, however, he informed me that "mental hygiene" was the term needed for the purpose in view. This was a happy choice—almost a stroke of genius in the devising of descriptive titles. Not only did "mental hygiene" describe the work as originally planned; it will continue to describe it accurately regardless of its growth.

It was Dr. Meyer who, because of his profound knowledge of the scientific, medical and social problems involved, did more than anyone else to place its initial work on a sound basis. After my manuscript and plans had been carefully examined by him, he sent me the following letter, which helped secure the co-operation of other psychiatrists and hospital officials whose support at that time was so essential to success:

NEW YORK CITY,
October 27, 1907.

To Whom It May Concern:

Since about a month ago, when Mr. C. W. Beers was introduced to me by Dr. Stewart Paton, I have had an unusual experience in finding in him a man not only without a chip on his shoulder, but one with a sound and worthy conviction that something must be done to meet one of the most difficult, but also lamentably neglected problems of sociological improvement. Unlike so many ex-patients to whose efforts we owe in many ways the preposterous forms of legislation concerning the insane and many prejudices about the hospitals, Mr. Beers has given us a description of his personal experiences, has pointed out his own impressions and suggestions for remedy and has asked for advice with an open mind, with such willingness to accept and use new conceptions of matters not broadly enough viewed by him before that it looks as if we had at last what we need: a man for a cause. The difficulties to be met are such as to be unsurmountable to anyone who has not the personal experience and instinctive foundation for what must equal a religious vow of devotion of his life to a task before which others have become opportunistic, if not indifferent.

Mr. Beers plans to subordinate his activity to a body of men and women who shall be chosen by a temporary Board of Trustees of the cause. It will be a difficult task to find the not very common level-headed and well-informed persons in various parts of the country capable of organizing the public conscience of the people. Neglected by physicians and dreaded by the fiscal authorities, the facts are not available to-day, except in fragments, mixed up with innumerable extraneous considerations; the hospitals are closed corporations, the press injudicious in inquiry and reform, and those capable of judgment unable to get the facts. The crying needs persist in the meantime. Instead of a Federal land fund (the 12,225,000 acres bill and ideal of Dorothea Dix, which failed of adoption by Congress) we must have a permanent survey of the facts and efficient handling of what is not prevented. Information must be put into practical form for communication and teaching, and brought home where it will tell; in opportunities of work and education for physicians and co-operation between our educational forces and those who labor for physical hygiene and prophylaxis.

Most of us are already under too many definite obligations to meet the call for devoted work for the maintenance of an organization as well as can Mr. Beers. In my judgment, he deserves the assistance which will make it possible for others to join in the work which will be one of the greatest achievements of this country and of this century—less sensational than the breaking of chains, but more far-reaching and also more exacting in labor.

A Society for Mental Hygiene, with a capable and devoted and judicious agent of organization, will put an end to the work of makeshift and short-sighted opportunism, and initiate work of prevention and of helping the existing hospitals to attain what they should attain, and further of adding those links which are needed to put an end to conditions almost unfit for publication. What officialism will never do alone must be helped along by an organized body of persons who have set their hearts on serious devotion to the cause.

If Mr. Beers gets the means to pursue his aim, he will secure the body which will guarantee proper judgment in a cause which has been a mere foster-child in the field of charitable donations merely because it seemed too difficult. Here is a man who is not afraid of the task. May he get the help to enable him to surround himself with the best wisdom of our Nation!

ADOLF MEYER.

Having thus secured needed moral support, my next task was to find financial support. In this Mr. Anson Phelps Stokes, at that time Secretary of Yale University, was one of my most active and helpful advisers. During the summer of 1907, he placed my manuscript before Mr. Frederick T. Gates, who then (before the Rockefeller Foundation was established) had almost exclusive charge of Mr. Rockefeller's philanthropies. Under date of October 30th, 1907, Mr. Gates wrote to me as follows:

" I am sending you herewith by express, at the request of Mr. Anson Phelps Stokes, the manuscript copy of your forthcoming work, which I have read with the deepest interest. I am very glad to learn from your recent letter to Mr. Stokes that you will publish soon. I have no doubt that your work will become a classic in its line, and if properly launched it will have a great and immediate popular success and produce a profound impression throughout the country."

Though the sending of my book to Mr. Gates at this time, and to others connected with Mr. Rockefeller's philanthropies, had no immediate effect on the financial situation, the fact remains that the Rockefeller Foundation, established subsequently, later contributed liberally to The National Committee for Mental Hygiene when its plans for surveys and special studies had been more definitely formulated.

As was to be expected, the first person I invited to become a member of the National Committee was William James. His acceptance follows:

CAMBRIDGE, November 23, 1907.

DEAR MR. BEERS:

I gladly consent to serve as an honorary trustee of your Society for Mental Hygiene.

I understand that our duties are primarily to let our names serve as evidence for our belief in the utility of such an auxiliary organization as your book proposes; secondarily to appoint the working committee, secretary, etc., when the thing reaches its working stage; and, finally, to act as general court of appeal in questions of policy about which the eventual active trustees might be in doubt.

I hope that most of the gentlemen whom you have thought of as possible trustees will feel as I do, that it is not only a duty, but a privilege to promote so humane a cause.

Sincerely yours,

WM. JAMES.

As the work in view was to be, in part, an educational campaign, I sought the support of some of the high officials of various universities. One of the first of these to accept membership in the National Committee was Professor Russell H. Chittenden, Director of the Sheffield Scientific School of Yale University, who wrote as follows, under date of December 5th, 1907:

"I am in receipt of your letter of December 4th, asking me to serve as one of the Honorary Trustees of the Society for Mental Hygiene, about to be established. Having read the manuscript of your forthcoming book, I have been much impressed by the story of your personal experiences, and I believe that much good can be accomplished for humanity by such a society as is contemplated. My knowledge of the underlying facts of your story, as related to me from time to time, at the date of their occurrence, by your brother, has given to me a realization of the truthfulness of the account of your personal experiences, and as a result I have been the more strongly impressed with the necessity for some movement tending to betterment of the conditions under which the insane are forced to live. A fuller understanding of methods of treatment such as can be fostered by a Society of the kind contemplated will do much toward improving the conditions of this unfortunate class. I trust that you will succeed in the efforts you are making."

Miss Julia C. Lathrop, then of Hull House, Chicago, later Chief of the Children's Bureau at Washington, wrote as follows, under date of January 2nd, 1908:

" I have devoted my spare time yesterday and to-day to reading the proof of your book. The autobiography is a most touching and appealing document. I earnestly hope that its admirable literary form may secure for it the wide reading so desirable for your purpose.

" I have felt for some time that a national society for the study of insanity and its treatment, from the social as well as the merely medical standpoint, should be formed. I am glad to follow in the line you have indicated and to have my name appear as one of the honorary trustees. I have talked with Miss Addams and she has agreed to the use of her name and will so inform you soon by letter.

" I see many indications of a strong revival of interest in the care of the insane and I cannot but believe that we shall within a few years see them treated generally as sick persons."

Dr. August Hoch, at one time Clinical Director at

Bloomingdale Hospital and later Director of the Psychiatric Institute of the New York State Hospitals, Ward's
Island, New York, through whose death a few years later
psychiatry lost one of its ablest leaders, wrote as follows,
under date of January 4th, 1908:

" Your letter reached me yesterday, and your book this
morning. I have just spent several hours reading the
latter, not only the parts to which you called my attention especially, but others as well. What I have read is
extremely interesting, not only psychologically, but in its
broad bearing as well, which you so fully appreciate.
There is no doubt that a society such as you propose
could do much to stimulate progress in the care and
treatment of the insane, as well as in the study and
teaching of psychiatry in this country. In all these
branches much is yet to be done. The time for your
undertaking is ripe.

" I highly appreciate your kindness in asking me to be
a trustee of the society and I gladly accept your offer,
assuring you at the same time that I shall cheerfully do
whatever lies in my power to assist in a cause in which I
am naturally deeply interested. I wish you success in
your undertaking."

A letter from Dr. William L. Russell, one of my earliest
advisers, who for a number of years served as Medical
Inspector of the New York State Hospital Commission,
and later became Medical Director of Bloomingdale
Hospital, read as follows, under date of January 16th,
1908:

" I need scarcely tell you that I have been intensely interested by the proof sheets of your book. I have read every word, and much I would gladly read again as, indeed, I certainly shall as soon as the work is published. You are quite right in thinking that an aroused public sentiment is necessary to effect any great improvements in the care of the insane. Without this, even earnest and enlightened workers cannot either obtain sufficient funds or eliminate selfishness and inefficiency in applying them. I am inclined to think that conditions in this State are rather better than in most others. We see, however, many defects, and I most sincerely trust that your efforts will be rewarded with success."

Early in January, 1908, largely upon the advice of Mr. George McAneny of New York, who had had wide experience as an organizer, it was decided to limit the membership of the society, make it a "Committee," rather than an "Association" with a general membership, and call it "The National Committee for Mental Hygiene." This was done, as the task in hand was a very special and, in many ways, delicate one. Furthermore, it was believed that the National Committee could not at first appeal for *general* members without, perhaps, diverting support that would be needed by the affiliated State Societies for Mental Hygiene which it planned to create.

Dr. Jacob Gould Schurman, for many years President of Cornell University, wrote as follows, under date of February 21st, 1908:

"I have now read all the pages which you set apart for my consideration. Let me say that they have interested me immensely. It is a most extraordinary thing to have a book written under such circumstances. If there is anything like it in the history of literature, I am not acquainted with it. And then, apart from the circumstance that we have in this volume an account of insanity by the sufferer himself, I have been greatly impressed with the author's lucidity of style, poise of judgment, and variety of knowledge outside his own special field, as well as the reformatory zeal with which he addresses himself to the problem of the intelligent and humane treatment of the insane.

"I should predict for the book a great success, merely as a piece of literature. I earnestly hope it will go a long way towards accomplishing the reformatory object to which it is dedicated. And if you think I can be of help in that direction, I shall certainly be very glad to accede to your request to serve as an honorary member of The National Committee for Mental Hygiene as outlined in your letter.

"With congratulations on your remarkable achievement, and with all good wishes for the success of the cause you have so much at heart, a cause with which I have had a little experience as Visitor of the New York State Charities Aid Association to the State Hospital at Willard, I remain, Very sincerely yours."

Dr. W. H. P. Faunce, President of Brown University, under date of February 24th, 1908, wrote as follows:

"Surely no one can read your manuscript without sympathy and without being fascinated by its clear presentation of a remarkable experience. I shall be glad to serve as one of your honorary trustees and hope that much good will come from the organization of The National Committee for Mental Hygiene."

Having secured the support of more than thirty representative men and women who were willing to serve as original members, I now felt secure in placing my book before the public. It was published on March 16th, 1908, and immediately attracted wide and favorable attention —if the reviews which appeared in more than one hundred newspapers and periodicals in this country and Great Britain may be taken as a criterion.

When "A Mind That Found Itself" was published, the projected National Committee for Mental Hygiene could have been founded at once. This, however, did not occur until February 19th, 1909, as it was thought best that a State Society should first be established by way of experiment on a smaller scale. Therefore the Connecticut Society for Mental Hygiene, which began its work on May 6th, 1908, was founded. While serving as its Executive Secretary and developing its work and financial resources, I continued to enlist support for the National Committee. With bound copies of my book now available and a collection of favorable opinions in my possession, my task became easier. That is, it was easy to gain moral support. Securing funds for the work, however, was difficult. I therefore continued my efforts to secure not only acceptances of membership, but opinions likely to influence potential donors.

That those who accepted membership in the National Committee became more interested in its plans the more they studied them, is indicated by Dr. Schurman's second letter of March 27th, 1908, which follows:

" I want to thank you very cordially for your book. I have now read it through. It is a wonderful volume— whether one considers its contents or the circumstances of its origin—and I find it intensely interesting. I found myself constantly admiring your literary gifts. And it is curious to reflect that they might never have come to a birth but for your domicile in a hospital for the insane. It is the last place in the world one would have selected as a school of liberal culture, yet in your case it meant a good deal more for your literary development than a college does for the generality of the students.·

" I need not say that the recital of the sufferings you endured deeply stirred my sympathy and at the same time aroused my indignation. It is clear there is need for reform. And I suppose no other man is so competent to undertake it as yourself.

" I take the liberty also of making a suggestion to yourself. You must not expect too sudden or too great a reform. Even good causes make their way slowly in this rough workaday world. You conceived your vocation as a reformer while you were a patient in the hospital. And as I read your book, I sometimes thought you entertained too extravagant hopes in regard to actual achievement. And so I feel like saying to you that you must not be disappointed if you find things moving slowly and gradually.

"You will not infer from what I have said that my own interest has been lessened by reading your book. On the contrary, it has been greatly increased, and I should be glad to aid so good a cause in any way in my power.

"With kindest regards and with congratulations on your production of so wonderful a book."

In acknowledging the receipt of a complimentary copy of my book, sent apparently at the psychological moment, the late Mr. Jacob A. Riis, under date of April 3rd, 1908, said:

"A woman, to whom a year or two ago I gave a lift that helped open the bars of the worse than prison in which she was confined without just cause, came into my office, the other day, with tears in her eyes and asked me to read your book, which she hailed as the promise of freedom for, she said, 'countless hundreds' of men and women as unfortunate as she was. And now to-day I found it upon my desk. I shall read it—I know already from the reviews what to expect—and I hope my poor friend is right. Meanwhile let me thank you very heartily for your gift. The world is so busy that it passes such suffering by unheeding because it 'has not time' to heed. If your book shall make it stop and pause, you have certainly rendered a service to your day that ought to be a monument indeed. *We will all help.*"

On April 10th, 1908, Mr. Riis wrote again, as follows:

" I have nearly finished your book and I am quite ready to help, for I see it is needed. My friend was right, and in losing your reason you found, I hope, ours for us in this pitiful matter."

Dr. M. Allen Starr, formerly Professor of Neurology at Columbia University, under date of April 11th, 1908, said:

" I have read with much interest your book which you so kindly sent me. It is a wonderful record, interesting from the psychological analysis of your mental condition, and most important as a protest against the bad nursing and inefficient medical direction prevalent in our asylums, especially the private ones. I have had only too many instances in my own experience which substantiate all the arraignment you make.

" You have my sincere sympathy for your sufferings— and if any definite steps are taken in the line of reform in which I can help, you will have my hearty support."

In seeking advice as to the best way to organize The National Committee for Mental Hygiene, I naturally consulted those in charge of the work of similar organizations. Dr. Livingston Farrand, then the Executive Secretary of The National Tuberculosis Association, now President of Cornell University, wrote as follows, under date of April 25th, 1908:

" I read your book last night. The best proof of my interest is that I finished it before going to bed. It is one of the most striking and convincing documents that I have ever seen.

" I have long felt that one of the most important phases of the present great movement in the direction of preventive medicine, and at the same time one of the most neglected, is that of mental hygiene. There is no doubt at all that very great good could be accomplished by an educational campaign dealing with the causes, prevention and adequate treatment of abnormal mental conditions. I do not believe that there could be a better means of engaging public interest than by making an attack upon the present shocking abuses in the treatment of the insane the peg upon which to hang the broad educational movement, which, after all, is the object of chief importance. After thinking over your propositions with some care, I see no reason why a national movement such as that you plan should not be entirely successful, and I am writing not only to thank you for the stimulus which your book has given me personally, but to assure you of hearty co-operation wherever possible in assisting such a movement. You have my very best wishes and renewed assurances of my co-operation."

On many occasions Dr. William H. Welch, the acknowledged leader of the medical profession in this country, Dean of the School of Hygiene at Johns Hopkins University, rendered great assistance. Under date of May 24th, 1908, he wrote as follows:

" I am glad to see that your efforts are beginning to be fruitful and that State and National Societies are to be formed to carry on the work.

" Your book, which you kindly sent me, I read with

great interest, and do not see how it can fail to be of great service. So far as I have observed, its reception both in the medical profession and by the general public has been sympathetic and encouraging. My copy has been loaned to several friends upon whom it has made a strong impression.

" I hope that you will continue to lay special emphasis upon the need of psychopathic hospitals and wards in connection with general hospitals, and especially with the university medical school. The greatest need is for improved care and treatment of early and curable cases of mental derangement and for border-land cases which can be prevented from passing into the insane state; also for better instruction of students and physicians in psychiatry. These needs will be met by psychiatric institutions in connection with general hospitals and university clinics better than by the familiar type of hospitals for the insane existing in this country."

Letters directly to the originator of a plan are apt to avoid the expression of mental reservations, if such are held by the writers. That the endorsements I had received were entirely genuine, however, could hardly be doubted after reading one that was not meant for my eyes, but which I was privileged to see and am now permitted to publish. It was sent under date of June 8th, 1908, by Mr. Wickliffe Rose, Director-General of The International Health Board of The Rockefeller Foundation, to the Rev. G. S. Dickerman, D.D., of New Haven, who later forwarded it to me. To quote:

" I read Mr. Beers's book with the most intense interest. To me it is a remarkable work. It impresses me as a bit of genuine literature, remarkably well written and revealing what is to me a new field of human experience. It is convincing to a degree and left me with the feeling that I should like to do something to remedy the conditions which he so vividly portrays.

" I am handing the book to friends, and hope to keep it traveling on its mission. I wish to thank you for calling my attention to it."

On July 10th, 1908, Dr. William H. Welch sent me a letter telling me that my book had played a part in the negotiations with Mr. Henry Phipps that led to the establishing of a Psychiatric Clinic at the Johns Hopkins Hospital. Thus I had the satisfaction of knowing that another of my objects, as presented in the first edition of my autobiography, was being achieved. Dr. Welch wrote in part as follows:

" I knew that none would rejoice more than you at the good news, and you may look upon the benefaction as one of the fruits of your efforts. Mr. Phipps became interested in the subject as the result of some remarks which I made at the time of a visit in May to see the workings of the dispensary for tuberculous patients which he has established in connection with the Johns Hopkins Hospital. These remarks were incidental and without thought of making an appeal to him. Shortly after his return to New York I received a letter saying that he was interested in what I had said about the need of improved care of the insane and desired further information. I then wrote him rather fully about the need of an institution such as those known in Germany as psychiatric clinics, and it will interest you to know that among other pamphlets, etc., I sent him my copy of your book, in which I marked many passages. His son, Mr. John S. Phipps, who was in his father's councils in this matter, also procured a copy of your book.

" When I told Mr. Phipps later how pleased you would be with his gift, especially as I could say that your book had influenced him, he himself expressed his pleasure at this. I told the reporters also about this feature, and mention of you and the book was made in the Baltimore papers, although not with as much detail as should have been the case, if they had reported my remarks more fully and accurately.

" I want you to know these facts, as they must be a great encouragement and gratification to you. The Phipps Psychiatric Clinic will, I think, be in a measure a fulfillment of your dreams."

As Mr. Phipps had shown so convincingly that he was interested in improving the treatment of mental diseases, he was invited to become a member of The National Committee for Mental Hygiene, which invitation he readily accepted. Here at last was a man who, when he understood the needs of the organization, would, I believed, give financial as well as moral support. Of moral support, the National Committee had a great deal; of financial support it had very little.

Indeed, its only financial support was that which I gave it indirectly through loans made to me, personally. Though I could ill afford to assume these obligations, the fact that the National Committee was not yet organized and had no funds for preliminary expenses made it necessary for me to do so. There was one loan, however, made to me by Professor William James which he converted into a contribution toward the initial expenses of organization. I had written Mr. James for advice regarding the advisability of asking Mr. Phipps to "take over" the debts I had incurred in organizing the National Committee and to trust me or the organization to repay him later. In giving my reasons for wishing to appeal to Mr. Phipps for assistance, I had unwittingly appealed to Mr. James, who, until now, had not been told of my debts. As I was innocent of any intention of securing help from Mr. James—one does not think of a university professor as being in a position to play the rôle of philanthropist—I found it possible to accept his gift, so generously offered in the following letter:

LONDON, August 16, 1908.

DEAR BEERS:

You seem to be doing splendidly, and I should be a caitif not to chip in to the taxes which you have so nobly piled upon your head. So I enclose to you an order on Lee Higginson & Co. of Boston for $1,000 to which extent I am only too willing to bleed for the cause. So you need not think of paying me till you become a millionaire yourself! I wish I could contribute more to relieve you of your indebtedness.   I can easily contribute this. In October I shall be home and glad to perform whatever duties my place as committeeman of the National Society may call for."

In a subsequent letter, Mr. James said he thought it proper for me to submit a statement of the organizing expenses to Mr. Phipps, but I finally decided not to do so, fearing I might in some way diminish the chance of securing from him, later, substantial support for the active work of the National Committee.

Though I usually wrote directly to those whose interest in the work I desired to enlist, on occasion I chose to present my request indirectly.   I used that method of approach when I invited His Eminence, the late Cardinal Gibbons, to serve as a member of the National Committee, for I knew that Dr. Welch was willing to support my request.   The following letters explain themselves:

807 St. Paul Street, Baltimore,
November 27, 1908.

To His Eminence, James, Cardinal Gibbons,

   Dear Cardinal Gibbons:

I am writing this line in the hope that you may become sufficiently interested in Mr. Clifford W. Beers and his remarkable book to be willing to encourage the national movement in behalf of improved care and treatment of the insane, and of better mental hygiene in general.

Mr. Beers's book, "A Mind That Found Itself," has

made a profound impression upon the medical profession as well as upon the general public.

You will observe that Mr. Beers has secured the support of eminent men in the movement which he has initiated. I feel confident that you would do a great service toward better care of the mentally afflicted, if you should be willing to lend your name in support of the national society to effect this purpose.

With the highest respect, I am

Faithfully yours,

WILLIAM H. WELCH.

ARCHDIOCESE OF MARYLAND

Chancery Office

408 NORTH CHARLES STREET,

November 18, 1909.

MY DEAR MR. BEERS:

Some months ago your work, "A Mind That Found Itself," fell into my hands. I read it with profound interest. To me it is a wonderful book. I scarcely remember ever having read anything which stirred me so deeply, or left upon my memory stronger or more vivid impressions. Its revelations of the sufferings and the tortures which the mentally afflicted have been doomed to undergo must touch even the hardest nature, and arouse compassion in every breast. Its purpose therefore is a noble one, and I have not the slightest hesitation in accepting your invitation to enroll my name among the members of The National Committee for Mental Hygiene, which is at present being organized.

Indeed this movement to mitigate the sufferings and agonies of this class of unfortunates commands my highest admiration and merits my heartiest support.

With sentiments of great esteem, I am

Yours very sincerely,

JAMES, CARD. GIBBONS.

As the pioneer State Society for Mental Hygiene (organized by me in Connecticut in May, 1908), had proved successful, plans for completing the organization of the National Committee were now decided upon. The formal founding occurred at a meeting held in New York City on February 19th, 1909. At this meeting, plans for work which had been formulated with great care during the preceding year and a half were adopted. To formulate these plans had not been an easy task, as there was no society in existence whose plan of work was sufficiently comprehensive to serve as a model for the work of the National Committee, nor, indeed, of the pioneer State Society of Connecticut, whose plans, by the way, were also made by the group that organized the National Committee. Work previously done, however, in behalf of the insane in New York by the State Charities Aid Association had made it easier to formulate part of the plans of the National Committee, namely, those features relating to State care and to after-care of the insane, in both of which fields the New York State Charities Aid Association had done the pioneer work so far as this country is concerned.

Instead of presenting in detail the original "plan of

work" of The National Committee for Mental Hygiene, I shall quote from an address delivered at Chautauqua in its behalf on August 11th, 1909, by the late Dr. Henry B. Favill, of Chicago, a leader in social work as well as in the field of medicine, who served as President of the Committee during its first years of existence:

"Why am I here to-day addressing you? Briefly it happens in this way. A man in Connecticut, Clifford W. Beers by name, was for three years confined in various hospitals for the insane, had various experiences, and ultimately, in 1903, regained his mental health. He came through that experience with an accurate memory and acute perception of everything that happened to him, a clear recollection of all the perverted mental processes that he went through, a keen sense of the misinterpretation to which his mental processes were exposed, a very temperate resentment at the unnecessary hardships and brutalities which he experienced, the outgrowth of a system and not of personal default, and all this he imparted in one of the most remarkable books of the age, 'A Mind That Found Itself.'

"With tremendous conviction and singleness of purpose he has devoted himself to the amelioration of social conditions as they bear upon the question of mental integrity. He has formed a society in Connecticut which is doing effective work. He conceived the idea of a National Committee which should do a comprehensive work in this direction. He selected a Board of Directors from all over the country. Incidentally,

I was made the President of the Committee. I am here speaking the first public word which has been uttered in its behalf.

"A proper question is, What is our programme? At the moment it is rather indefinite, and yet in a general way I can say to you what we propose to do.

"In the first place we need money to carry on an effective work. We hope to get that from some source. As the next step, which seems logically to be the last step, which we shall probably pursue, we propose actively to take up what is known as 'after-care of the insane.' That means the establishing of relations between patients who are about to be discharged as cured, or partially cured, and their outside work, establishing a connection which will continue a wise supervision out into their social relations. The value of this is twofold.

"In the first place, its tendency is to prevent relapse by foreseeing conditions unfavorable to the individual and preventing their harmful operation. In this way probably a very large percentage of the relapses can be prevented.

"But, more than this, and probably far more important than this, will be the relationship which becomes thereby established with the family and group and entire social circle of the individual.

"In establishing a harmonious relation in this way there is no doubt that a great deal of impending mental disaster can be averted. It is one of the ways in which early contact with mental disturbances can be secured.

"Please to realize the difficulty in this point. Supposing, without any entering wedge, we undertake to go to a family which we know to be more or less vulnerable and say, 'You have a bad family make-up, your family history is bad, you are all liable to go to pieces mentally, we want to fix it.' Imagine, if you can, anything more impossible to accomplish than results upon such a basis.

"On the other hand, if you can go into that situation naturally, carefully and with a sympathetic connection already established through an actual patient, there is practically no limit to the access which can be secured. Whatever results are possible from such early access can be achieved. Those are the merits of 'after-care.'

"Next, our programme is education, spreading broadcast, as we may, correct ideas about insanity, mental balance, mental hygiene, right living.

"And next, we shall attempt to effect legislation, so to alter the laws and the procedure as to fit in with this fundamental conception of mental unsoundness.

"As a preliminary to that legislation, we must have popular opinion. Legislation cannot go much beyond public opinion, and it is our desire, and it will be our effort, to create public opinion as fast and as widely as we may.

"And now the question is, What do we want from you? The answer is simple,—merely a hearing, merely a fair judgment, as to the soundness of what we set forth, merely a sense of its importance, and growing out of that a conviction as to your relation to it.

"We want a hearing and we feel confident that as a

result of a hearing we shall found an individual conviction on the part of practically everyone as to his obliga-
tion to help where he can.

" I do not hesitate to say that of all the great public
movements that are going on for the correction, the
amelioration of social conditions, there is none more
important nor more deserving of your earnest attention."

At the founding meeting of the National Committee in
1909, it was confidently believed that funds for the
beginning of active work would soon be secured. A year
later, however, no gifts having been received, how to
finance the work became the chief topic of discussion at
the second annual meeting, held on April 9th, 1910. The
advice given at that time by Dr. Favill, who was then
president, proved to be prophetic. To quote from his
remarks:

" It seems to me very clear that the question of policy
with us at this moment is essentially a question of finance.
If we had money enough, we would all be agreed that it
was best to organize efficiently with well-paid officials
and go into a comprehensive campaign with which we
could make good—educationally, institutionally, and
illustratively. If, on the other hand, we have not
money enough, the most that we could accomplish would
be a flash in the pan. Personally, I have a very strong
feeling that an appeal to any considerable number of
the public would be futile at this moment. Prof.
Fisher has stated part of it, namely, that the public

does not understand insanity. I am quite prepared from my personal experience to state another part of it and that is that the public does not yield money to organizations except under a very definite and protracted pressure and then only upon a presentation of things so cogent as to be convincing in some degree or other—not only of their importance, but from personal relation—to the individuals in question.

" I am raising money or helping to raise money for many organizations and I am thoroughly convinced of the difficulties encountered in popular subscriptions. Aside from the question of difficulty, however, I am as much convinced that the smaller the source of our money at first, the safer we are, just as I am convinced that in the long run the wider our financial foundations, the safer we are. Any co-operation or support to this movement at this time requires vision. If the individual furnishing the money has not the vision, he must have faith in a few individuals who have vision and it has got to be the sort of faith which will go on not only one or two, but perhaps three or four or five years before results can be achieved sufficient really to be regarded as tangible and demonstrable results. The public will not stand that sort of procrastination. The public or any small portion of the public will not be able to have loyalty and adherence to any proposition of this kind, to be counted upon for support. I believe that we have got to find a man who will come into this situation with a fund or a guarantee, based upon a conviction, instilled into him by those who have the power, as to the importance of the work and the necessarily protracted character of the preliminary operations. I think that our Finance Committee is the crux of the situation and I predict, without any pessimism, that it will be found that unless a very limited focus of financial support can be made, we will be a year hence in not a very different position from what we are now. That is my feeling in the matter and, consequently, I regard our deliberations to-day as being essentially the establishment of a financial policy which, if it can be successful, will by that very fact establish to a large extent our future organic policy."

Dr. Favill was right. A year later, though The New York Foundation had given three thousand dollars to the National Committee, no large gift, insuring the continuance of work on an active basis for a period of years, had been secured. Failure to find the needed support was not occasioned by any defect in the plan for work. The trouble was that the "man of vision," referred to by Dr. Favill, had not been found. In November, 1911, however, he revealed himself. Mr. Henry Phipps proved to be the long-hoped-for patron. He offered his gift while talking with Dr. William H. Welch. No one had asked him to contribute. That the gift was spontaneously offered was characteristic of Mr. Phipps; for he had a way of sensing needs and taking the initiative in meeting them. His confirmatory letter sent to Dr. Welch read as follows:

NEW YORK CITY,
November 4, 1911.

DEAR DR. WELCH,

For some time past I have been thinking of what I could do toward ameliorating the condition of the insane in public and private institutions and I shall be very glad, as mentioned to you this morning, if you will accept Fifty Thousand Dollars ($50,000) and appoint suitable parties to carry out such views as you may have on the subject.

I will send you a check whenever it is required.

Sincerely yours,
HENRY PHIPPS.

Though Mr. Phipps at this time was a member of The National Committee for Mental Hygiene he, like most other members, did not know much about its work—for the simple reason that it had done no active work. But he had read my story and I have reason to believe that its effect upon him, of which he spoke to others later, perhaps inspired his gift. His desire, as stated in his letter, was "to ameliorate conditions among the insane in public and private institutions," which was one of the chief purposes of The National Committee for Mental Hygiene. As might have been expected, Dr. Welch recommended that the $50,000 be given to that organization, which was soon done.

Shortly after the announcement of Mr. Phipps's gift to the National Committee, I received from him a note in

which he said: "I should like to take you motoring when
you can find time to call, giving me notice of a day or
two.   We could have an interesting talk."

' A week later I spent an afternoon with Mr. Phipps.
While motoring he talked about my book and showed
lively appreciation of the service I had rendered in publishing it and in organizing The National Committee for
Mental Hygiene.   Evidently my story had given Mr.
Phipps the impression that one who had once suffered a
mental breakdown should not, after recovery, work too
hard and, above all, should not be subjected to worries.
I assured him that I had proved that I had a high degree
of resistance both to the strain of work and to such
worries as had been involved in carrying my project
forward.   But Mr. Phipps seemed not to be convinced,
for he said, "How much would it take to keep you
from worrying?"   This was indeed a baffling question
put to a man in debt on account of the work — by
a man of great wealth, famous for his generosity,
who had already shown interest in the project.   I told
Mr. Phipps that as I was his guest it hardly seemed
proper for me to discuss my personal affairs and needs.
"I had you come to see me for the purpose of discussing
them," he said.   "Would five thousand dollars be of
use?   I want you to have it as a buttress—for a 'rainy
day.'"   As the period from January 1st, 1907, when I
abandoned my business career and an assured salary to
give my whole time to the publishing of my book and
the organizing of the National Committee, had, in a
financial sense, been one continuous "rainy day," I at

once accepted this golden bolt from the blue that cleared my financial skies. The next day I received the following note from Mr. Phipps:

1063 FIFTH AVENUE,
December 12, 1911.

DEAR MR. BEERS:

It gives me much pleasure to ask you to accept the enclosed check for five thousand dollars ($5,000), to be exclusively for your own use: nothing to do with The National Committee for Mental Hygiene.

Trusting it may add to your pleasure,

Yours sincerely,

HENRY PHIPPS.

This was, indeed, a timely gift, for I had expended more than ten thousand dollars in publishing my book and organizing the National Committee, eight thousand of which represented money borrowed of banks, and of a few individuals who believed in my ultimate success. Through a partial reimbursement secured by the National Committee for the specific purpose and previously voted me by it on account of expenses incurred in its behalf, both before and while serving as its temporary secretary, I had already paid three thousand dollars of my debts. With Mr. Phipps's unexpected gift I was now able to pay all other debts. For the first time in nearly five years, I owed no one a dollar on account of my work. I also had the satisfaction of knowing that my judgment regarding the feasibility of my project had at last been vindicated, for not only was

I out of debt, but the National Committee had funds sufficient for at least three years of active work. Soon afterwards I was appointed Secretary with a real, if modest, salary.

Many fortunate occurrences have contributed to the success of The National Committee for Mental Hygiene, chief among them being the securing of Dr. Thomas W. Salmon as its Medical Director when the active work was begun in March, 1912. Having been an officer of the United States Public Health Service in charge of the mental examination of immigrants at Ellis Island for several years, and a member of the medical staff of a State Hospital and later Chairman of the Board of Alienists of the New York State Hospital Commission, Dr. Salmon was able to place the work of the National Committee on an effective basis within a short time. During the ten years that he has served as Medical Director, virtually all of the important plans for work have been visioned, formulated and directed by him, especially with reference to special studies, surveys and war and reconstruction work, the most difficult of the many activities of the organization. Fortunate, too, has the National Committee been in having among its most active members leaders in psychiatry, neurology, psychology, general medicine, education, finance and social work in this country who have given generously of their time in serving as members of its inner comittees.

The National Committee was now a going concern. The tendency of the work to find itself occupying a wider and wider field is illustrated by an address delivered in

September, 1912, by Dr. Llewellys F. Barker, former Professor of Medicine at Johns Hopkins University, who for several years served as President of the National Committee. To quote in part:

" It is right that, in an International Congress of Hygiene and Demography, the subject of Mental Hygiene should have especial representation. Though assigned, as a sub-section, to the section on the Hygiene of Infancy and Childhood, thus emphasizing its relations to inheritance on the one hand and to the early environmental period of the individual on the other, it might almost equally well, for other reasons, have been made a sub-division in anyone of the main groups of the Congress. Indeed, so important is this sub-division for the welfare of individuals, of families, of communities, of nations, and of the human race in general, and so widespread its ramifications, that committees on the organization of future Congresses might well consider the establishment of an additional main section, devoted entirely to Mental Hygiene.

" By a campaign for mental hygiene is meant a continuous effort directed toward conserving and improving the minds of the people, in other words, a systematic attempt to secure human brains, so naturally endowed and so nurtured, that people will think better, feel better, and act better, than they do now. Such a campaign was not to be expected before the rise of modern medicine. For only with this rise have we come to look upon states of mind as directly related to states of brain, to view insanity as disordered brain-function, and to recognize

in imbecility, and in crime, the evidences of brain-defect.
The imbecile, the hysterical, the epileptic, the insane,
and the criminal, were formerly regarded sometimes as
saints or prophets, sometimes as wizards or witches, often
as the victims of demoniac possession, on the one hand
to be revered or worshipped, or, on the other, to be
burned or otherwise tortured. Now, such unfortunates
are looked upon as patients with disordered or defective
nervous systems, proper subjects of medical care; some
of them are curable; some are incurable, but still educable
to social usefulness; a part of them are socially so worth-
less, harmful or dangerous as to make their exclusion
from general society necessary, or desirable. It is but a
short step from such a reformation of ideas to the realization that less marked deviations from normal thought,
feeling, or behavior, are also evidences either of brains
defective from the start, or made abnormal in function
by bad surroundings or by bodily disease. As examples
of such marked abnormalities may be mentioned those
met with in children who are difficult to educate, in
young people arraigned in the Juvenile Courts, in adults,
who, inadequate to the strains of life, crowd our hospitals or sanitoria on account of 'nervous' or 'mental'
breakdown, or who, owing to anomalies of character and
conduct, provide material for the news columns of the
sensational press.

Modern medicine has taught us to recognize that the
conditions necessary for a good mind include, first, the
inheritance of such germ-plasm from one's progenitors
as will yield a brain capable of a high grade of develop-

ment to individual and social usefulness, and, secondly, the protection of that brain from injury and the submission of it to influences favorable to the development of its powers. Now if these doctrines of modern medicine be true, the general problems of mental hygiene become obvious; broadly conceived, they consist, first, in providing for the birth of children endowed with good brains, denying, as far as possible, the privilege of parenthood to the manifestly unfit who are almost certain to transmit bad nervous systems to their offspring—that is to say, the problem of eugenics; and second, in supplying all individuals, from the moment of fusion of the parental germ-cells onward, and whether ancestrally well begun or not, with the environment best suited for the welfare of their mentality.

" The natural sciences are built up by the gradual discovery of causal relationships; and physicians and psychologists have, since the time of Pinel, gone far in the establishment of the laws underlying normal and abnormal phenomena of mind. From the conviction that a proper application of the facts already discovered can vastly improve the mental powers of our people, decreasing to a large extent the prevalence of mental defect and mental disease, has come the impulse to arouse public opinion in favor of a definite plan for mental hygiene. This impulse, thanks to the initiative of a layman, Clifford W. Beers (now Secretary of the National Committee), author of 'A Mind That Found Itself,' whose personal sufferings led him on recovery to devote himself to the cause of mental hygiene, and who enlisted the co-operation of a group of representative men and women, has found expression in the voluntary formation of a National Committee for Mental Hygiene."

As pointed out by Dr. Barker, we immediately found that the usefulness of such an auxiliary organization was bound to spread from fields mapped out to new fields not originally included in the scope of the work. Though written much later, a letter from Dr. Walter E. Fernald, Superintendent of The Massachusetts School for Feebleminded at Waverley (who has long been recognized as the leader in the field of mental deficiency in this country), shows how we had all builded better than we knew. Under date of November 27th, 1916, Dr. Fernald said:

"Had you begun your work with the express purpose of rendering help to the mentally defective, instead of to the insane, you could not have planned an agency better fitted to cope with the difficulties of the problem of mental deficiency than is The National Committee for Mental Hygiene.

"It has been my privilege to witness and, in various ways, to participate in the growth of the now widespread movement in behalf of the mentally defective. At first this was a slow growth, but during the past ten years—and especially during the past five—it has been one of the most striking social developments of the day. Many individuals, groups and forces have contributed to this fortunate result. The National Committee for Mental Hygiene felt the force of this movement within one year of the time it began its active work in 1912 and wisely began then to bring into its membership physicians who had special knowledge of the problem of mental deficiency. As in all new fields—when pioneer work is done by many unrelated groups and by zealous individuals—there was great danger that propaganda might out-run dependable data and that unwise plans, policies and laws relating to State care of the mentally defective might be hastily adopted in many States. This danger, however, has been averted, and I believe that The National Committee for Mental Hygiene and its affiliated State Societies are destined to continue to influence, along wise and effective lines, the management of all phases of the great problem of mental deficiency."

So many people fail to appreciate that the mental hygiene movement is of vital concern to *everybody* that it seems advisable to present an excerpt from an article that appeared in *Mental Hygiene* (July, 1921), by Dr. C. Macfie Campbell, Professor of Psychiatry at Harvard University, and Chairman of the Committee on Education of The National Committee for Mental Hygiene. To quote:
"Mental hygiene is not concerned merely with those serious forms of mental disorder which require treatment in State hospitals; it is concerned with those other forms of mental disorders which do not necessarily mean the removal of the individual from his ordinary social environment. A disorder is a mental disorder if its roots are

mental. A headache indicates a mental disorder if it comes because one is dodging something disagreeable. A pain in the back is a mental disorder if its persistence is due to discouragement and a feeling of uncertainty and a desire to have sick benefit, rather than to put one's back into one's work. Sleeplessness is a mental disorder if its basis lies in personal worries and emotional tangles. Many mental reactions are indications of poor mental health, although they are not usually classified as mental disorders. Discontent with one's environment may be a mental disorder, if its cause lie, not in some external situation, but in personal failure to deal with one's emotional problems. Suspicion, distrust, misinterpretation, are mental disorders when they are the disguised expression of repressed longings, into which the patient has no clear insight. Stealing sometimes indicates a mental disorder, the odd expression of underlying conflicts in the patient's nature. The feeling of fatigue sometimes represents, not overwork, but discouragement, inability to meet situations, lack of interest in the opportunities available. Unsociability, marital incompatibility, alcoholism, an aggressive and embittered social attitude, may all indicate a disorder of the mental balance, which may be open to modification. Acute phenomena characterized by unreasoning emotional reactions, such as lynching and other mob reactions, waves of popular suspicion sweeping over a country, may be looked upon as transitory disorders. The same factors that are involved in these familiar reactions play an important part in the development of insanity."

THE gift of $50,000 from Mr. Henry Phipps provided for the first three years of work. In 1914 no funds for use beyond that year were in sight. This crisis was met in the following way. A copy of "A Mind That Found Itself" was sent to each of one hundred people of wealth, known to be liberal contributors to worthy work. With each inscribed copy of the book a letter of appeal was sent, asking for pledges to cover a period of years. Few had faith in the scheme and one adviser even predicted that the appeals would go the common route of circular letters—into the wastebasket. I ventured to predict that the book would keep or lift some of them out of it, and events justified my judgment.

Two of the letters brought surprising results. Mrs. William K. Vanderbilt and the late Mrs. Elizabeth Milbank Anderson responded with pledges to the value of $2,500 each, and asked me to call and tell them in person about the work. As the most difficult task of one who has an unproved plan to present is to secure interviews with potential donors, this was a very fortunate result. Mrs. Anderson soon gave $10,000 and Mrs. Vanderbilt $4,500 for use during 1915; and a little later these two benefactors each pledged $10,000 a year for the four years ending in 1919. This backlog of support gave us time in which to secure from others gifts for general and specific purposes during those years. Thus was the second financial crisis met. The copies of my book which had kept at least two of my early letters of appeal out of the wastebasket had brought to the National Committee gifts amounting to nearly $100,000. Indeed, the copy sent to Mrs. Anderson may be said to have brought to its treasury a quarter of a million dollars, for her gifts, and her bequest of $100,000 (this generous friend died on February 23rd, 1921), total that amount. In addition, Mrs. Anderson gave a conditional pledge of $100,000 toward endowment, as described later.

Other liberal *individual* contributors have been Mrs. E. H. Harriman, who has given or pledged $45,000 in the form of annual gifts of $5,000 each, largely for work in mental deficiency, in which field Mrs. Harriman and her daughter, Mrs. Rumsey, were among the pioneers in this country; and Miss Anne Thomson, who gave $15,000 for initiating war work. Toward general expenses, Mr. V. Everit Macy has given or pledged $10,000; and Mrs. Willard Straight, Mr. George F. Baker, Jr., Mr. Cyrus H. McCormick, Dr. and Mrs. Walter B. James, Mr. Robert S. Brewster, Mrs. Helen Hartley Jenkins, Mr. Nicholas F. Brady, Mr. Adolph and Mr. Sam A. Lewisohn and Miss Mabel Choate, have given or pledged approximately $5,000 each. Several others have given $1,000 at intervals, and still others have contributed smaller amounts. The Rockefeller Foundation, the New York Foundation, the Commonwealth Fund and the Milbank Memorial Fund have contributed, from time to time, largely for special purposes.

All told, not more than fifty individuals have contributed to the National Committee since it was founded in 1909. The support of a few, rather than of the many, during the early years of a philanthropy is often desirable, as Dr. Favill says in his remarks that appear on a preceding page. But, as he also points out, there comes a time when a wider basis of support is not only desirable, but indispensable to the healthy growth of any work. That time has now come. A work which benefits the whole public deserves to be supported by public-spirited people of wealth in all cities and in all States. Thus far, nearly all of the support of the National Committee has come from one city and one State, New York.

Concerted efforts are now being made to secure adequate funds for maintenance, development, and endowment. The work and the needs of the National Committee are being presented to individuals and to groups throughout the country. People who have never before learned in detail of the work are to be given the chance to contribute, or pledge future gifts, in proportion to their resources, their belief in the need for organized mental hygiene work, and their faith in the National Committee. In this way, it is hoped that this organization, which champions great classes who need help (but have never yet received what they deserve), may be placed in a position to give that help promptly and on a scale in keeping with the demands. Funds are needed, not alone for endowment, but for general expenses. For, unless an adequate staff of skilled workers can be maintained, gifts for special purposes, such as surveys, studies and demonstrations, cannot be administered with full effectiveness.

The letter from Mrs. Anderson, which opened the quest for endowment, speaks for itself. To quote:

New York City,
November 29, 1919.

OTTO T. BANNARD, ESC., Treasurer,
  The National Committee for Mental Hygiene, Inc.,
    New York City.

DEAR MR. BANNARD:

I am very much interested in the effort about to be made to raise an adequate endowment, the income of which will be available to perpetuate the work of The National Committee for Mental Hygiene, Inc. I discussed this matter at some length with Mr. Beers and I am now prepared to pledge the sum of $100,000 upon the condition that your Committee will use its best efforts to raise an additional sum of $900,000 to the end that the Committee will have at its disposal an endowment of at least $1,000,000, a sum which, to my mind, is clearly needed if the full benefits of the undertaking are to be realized. . . .

I am well satisfied with all that has been accomplished since Mr. Beers first stirred my interest in the work and I feel that we all owe him a debt of gratitude for the important part he has taken in focussing public attention on a subject of such vital concern to the community. I earnestly hope that your efforts to place the work on a permanent foundation will meet with complete success.

Yours very truly,
ELIZABETH MILBANK ANDERSON.

Under the pledge of Mrs. Anderson, a liberal time for completing the endowment is given; and of the amount pledged, $50,000 becomes payable as soon as $450,000 from other sources has been secured.

Mrs. Anderson was keenly interested in the plan for securing an endowment, and she and I once discussed the possibility of securing gifts for the National Committee through bequests. She said that if others found pleasure, as she did, in making a will, it would be perfectly proper to ask people of wealth to consider providing for bequests to The National Committee for Mental Hygiene. As the subject of making a will is a delicate one and as probably few people (except the lawyers) find pleasure in drawing up wills, I have never yet had the temerity to discuss possible bequests for the National Committee with people who can afford to make them. Nevertheless, I have courage enough to write as I now do and thus bring the subject, in a general way, to the attention of readers who may be in a position to remember the National Committee in their wills, along with other incorporated organizations engaged in work of a philanthropic nature.

Mrs. Anderson bequeathed $100,000, unconditionally, to the National Committee. It is planned to call this the Elizabeth Milbank Anderson Fund of the National Committee and include it in the Committee's endowment. Recently a bequest of a few thousand dollars was received under the will of the late Margaret W. Gage of Cambridge, Massachusetts. In 1917, Miss Gage wrote as follows: "Will you kindly send me some printed matter describing the work of your society? I want to give a small bequest in my will to help in the prevention and cure of insanity and I want to know where is wisest to apply the bequest." A copy of "A Mind That Found Itself," and other publications descriptive of the National Committee were sent to Miss Gage, who later wrote that she was "convinced of its reliability and its good work." If a bequest could follow in this instance without any further correspondence or an interview, is it not reasonable to expect that the information set forth in this book may inspire similar action on the part of others?

Enough has been said to show that the success of the work of The National Committee for Mental Hygiene is assured. So great are the needs, however, and so wide in scope is the work that gifts for its maintenance, development and for endowment, will continue to be needed. Though it is not necessary, I am sure, to present opinions showing that liberal support for the work is deserved, I shall, nevertheless, present a letter from Dr. Charles W. Eliot, President Emeritus of Harvard University, who became a Vice-President of The National Committee for Mental Hygiene even before its active work was begun. He sent it to me after reading the page proofs of part of the revised 4th Edition of my autobiography.

CAMBRIDGE, MASS.
17 January, 1917.

DEAR MR. BEERS:

I am glad to hear that you are about to publish a revised edition of "A Mind That Found Itself," which will contain an account of the organizing of The National

Committee for Mental Hygiene. Your part in creating that Committee was so important that an account of it will be an entirely appropriate addition to your book, which had a highly interesting autobiographical character, and owed much of its immediate influence to that quality.

I have just had the pleasure of reading the proofs of your account of the creation of The National Committee for Mental Hygiene; and want to congratulate you at once on the friends and supporters you have found in the prosecution of your difficult enterprise, and to suggest that the work of the Committee is sure to be permanent, and therefore should be supported on a permanent endowment. The work of the Committee now divides itself into original inquiries or surveys, popular education concerning the care and treatment of the insane and the preventable causes of mental disease and deficiency, and the organizing and advising of agencies (federal, state and local) for promoting the objects for which the Committee labors. All three of these objects have a permanent character; although the function of inquiring and surveying may later take the form of inspecting. A permanent work of this sort should be supported by an adequate endowment.

Thus far in the life of the National Committee its resources have been of a temporary nature, supplied chiefly by such very unusual givers as Mr. Henry Phipps, Mrs. Elizabeth Milbank Anderson, and Mrs. William K. Vanderbilt, and the Rockefeller Foundation. I congratulate you that your Board of Directors has already voted that an endowment fund be raised; and I wish you prompt success in obtaining that endowment. You have already been so successful in enlisting both sympathy and pecuniary support for your cause that I anticipate for you success in this new undertaking.

Among your friends and supporters, the most interesting and remarkable personage, to my thinking, was William James. His letters to you about your work, and his gift of a thousand dollars to your cause—for him a very large gift—must have been very delightful to you, and helpful also. They moved me very much as I read them last evening; and I hope that they will move to aid you some among his numerous friends and admirers who can afford the luxury and enjoy the privilege of liberally endowing worthy and competent agencies for promoting human welfare.

Sincerely yours,
CHARLES W. ELIOT.

Except during the first three years (1912–1915), before its work had outgrown its financial resources, The National Committee for Mental Hygiene has never had funds adequate to the needs during any given year. Despite this handicap, remarkable results have been attained. The next chapter tells of the accomplishments and indicates what can be done when adequate funds are available.

II

TEN YEARS OF WORK

As the work of The National Committee for Mental Hygiene is for the most part of a medical nature, the following account of its activities has been taken largely from statements prepared from time to time by Dr. Thomas W. Salmon, its Medical Director during the "ten years of work."

When the funds were secured that enabled the Committee to commence active work in 1912, the outlook for a successful movement in this new field of health and social work presented many disheartening features. While the treatment of other disorders had been practically revolutionized during the last one hundred years and, during the last twenty years, the popular distrust of general hospitals had practically disappeared, the treatment of mental diseases was just emerging from a very long period of neglect and inhumanity. Even among educated persons in the most civilized countries mental diseases were often regarded as visitations coming from unknown causes and the insane as persons to be treated with a certain consideration because they were still human beings—but quite beyond the possibility of restoration to health. In medical schools (except in one or two foreign countries), psychiatry occupied a place

too inconspicuous to give even the most thoughtful
student more than an inkling of the vast field of mental
medicine that existed.   Great health movements which
were avowedly general in their character gave no recognition at all to the fact that mental disease as well as
physical disease might possibly be prevented.   There
existed no course of instruction in mental hygiene in
any school, college or university and the literature on
the preventive aspects of psychiatry was limited to a
few dozen titles, many of which had little or no practical
bearing upon the subject.   Excellent reasons could have
been advanced for deciding not to enter such an un-
promising field.   It was largely because of a realization
of the great suffering which accompanies mental disease
that those who organized the Committee decided not to
put off making an attempt to reduce its aggregate
amount.   The notoriously slow growth of a more
rational public attitude toward mental illness and the
hygiene of mind seemed to them to call for prompt
action rather than to justify delay.

With the gift of $50,000 from Mr. Henry Phipps, which
maintained the work for the first three years, The
National Committee for Mental Hygiene, in March, 1912,
entered the field of organized preventive medicine.   It
seemed, however, to those who were responsible for its
pioneer work, that it would be idle to attempt to popularize information regarding the preventable causes of
mental disease while the subject itself was one which
could hardly be discussed because of the prejudice and
misinformation that were so prevalent.   At a time when

a large proportion of persons suffering from some of the most serious of all diseases were abandoned almost from the earliest appearance of symptoms to the care of ignorant custodians, when the law itself placed a stigma of hopelessness and pauperism upon the very names of the disorders from which they suffered and made people shrink from acknowledging their existence, and when the background of prison, poorhouse and asylum was in many States scarcely disappearing into the past, it would have been useless to advocate the recognition in childhood of traits tending toward mental disease, the establishment of mental hygiene clinics or the wide application of recently discovered facts in mental medicine to such social problems as the management of delinquency, the classification and training of prisoners and the study of industrial problems. For this reason, the work of the first three years was almost wholly devoted to the attempt to promote, by means of carefully planned popular education, the growth of that better attitude toward mental illness and its problems which was already coming into existence with the general spread of humanitarian ideals.

In the autumn of 1912 an International Congress on Hygiene and Demography was held in Washington. A mental hygiene exhibit was carefully prepared during the preceding summer with the aid of many experts in special fields of work. The incidence, cost and social significance of mental disease and mental deficiency and the fields of preventive effort were presented in a graphic and striking form to a large number of persons engaged in health and social work. This exhibit won a Diploma of Superior Merit. At the International Congress, mental hygiene appeared for the first time in a program of meetings devoted to hygiene and sanitation and the "Mental Hygiene Movement," as a newly organized endeavor to combat disease, received formal recognition in the United States. Later the exhibit was shown at a series of mental hygiene meetings in various cities throughout the country. At the Panama Pacific Exposition at San Francisco, it was awarded a Grand Prize.

Even with the limited funds available during the first three years, an attempt was made by means of surveys to ascertain the actual conditions under which mental diseases were treated in several States and to acquaint the people of those States with the facts disclosed. These demonstrations opened the way for the important survey work done later.

The most critical period of the newly launched work occurred in 1914 when the single appropriation (the gift of Mr. Phipps), upon which work had been commenced three years earlier, was all but expended. The question in the minds of all those who had shared in the hopes and fears of the initial work was, " Has it been demonstrated that mental hygiene constitutes a practical field of effort?" The National Committee made no attempt to advertise itself, but tried simply to state the most urgent problems of mental hygiene as they appeared. As a result of the presentation of the field and of the needs of the organization, Mrs. Elizabeth Milbank Anderson and

Mrs. William K. Vanderbilt, as stated elsewhere, tided the National Committee over this crisis in its affairs by contributing generously toward general expenses. Soon afterwards the Rockefeller Foundation began to contribute liberally for special studies and surveys.

The year 1916 was one of rapid development. Among the important studies undertaken during that year were that of the Psychiatric Clinic at Sing Sing Prison; a survey of the incidence of mental deficiency in Nassau County, New York; and surveys of the care of mental diseases in the States of Georgia, Connecticut, Louisiana, Pennsylvania, Indiana, Colorada and California, and in the cities of Scranton and New York. Owing to the rapid growth of its work in behalf of the feebleminded, the National Committee appointed at this time a Committee on Mental Deficiency, of which Dr. Walter E. Fernald became chairman. Soon afterwards surveys of mental deficiency were begun in several States.

The study at Sing Sing Prison demonstrated the vital importance of the mental factors involved in crime and delinquency. As a result of the demonstration made at Sing Sing, the need for psychiatric clinics in connection with prisons, reformatories and courts is now generally recognized. With funds made available by the Rockefeller Foundation, assistance was given to the Psychiatric Clinic at the Childrens Court in New York City; the Police Department of a great city was assisted in organizing a Psychopathic Clinic; and a study of all the children in a truant school in one city was made. These activities recently led to the adoption of a plan for a Division on the Prevention of Juvenile Delinquency as a part of the work of the National Committee.

During these first four years of work, the organizing of affiliated societies and committees for mental hygiene had been brought about in fifteen States. These agencies began to arouse interest in mental hygiene problems and several instituted social service in behalf of mental patients and their relatives.

In 1917, the publication of a quarterly magazine, *Mental Hygiene*, was begun by the National Committee. This official journal of the organization and of the movement in this country has done much to popularize the subject of mental hygiene. Its active editor is Dr. Frankwood E. Williams, an Associate Medical Director, who is assisted by an editorial board. A description of the magazine and a list of publications of the National Committee appear in a later chapter. The reduced facsimile of a cover of the magazine on the opposite page gives an idea of its general contents.

WAR WORK

Then came the war. The experience of our Allies showed those who had carefully studied medico-military problems since 1914 that mental and nervous diseases, especially the functional nervous disorders, termed "psycho-neuroses," play an enormous part in modern warfare. Even before the United States had formally entered the war it was realized that it was the duty of The National Committee for Mental Hygiene to lead the way in preparing to meet this new health problem of

MENTAL HYGIENE

VOL. V   JULY, 1921   NO. 3

CONTENTS

PUBLISHED QUARTERLY BY

THE NATIONAL COMMITTEE FOR MENTAL HYGIENE, INC.

PUBLICATION OFFICE: 27 COLUMBIA ST., ALBANY, N. Y.

EDITORIAL OFFICE: 370 SEVENTH AVENUE, NEW YORK CITY

Two Dollars a Year   Fifty Cents a Copy

military service.   A committee, consisting of Dr. Pearce
Bailey, Dr. Stewart Paton and Dr. Salmon, presented
to the Surgeons General of the Army and of the Navy
plans for the organization of military neuro-psychiatric
units, the early treatment and examination of mental
patients and the elimination of recruits suffering from
mental diseases, mental deficiency and nervous disorders.

At the request of General Gorgas, this committee of
the National Committee visited the Texas border in
March, 1917, to study the neuro-psychiatric problems
presented in that relatively small mobilization of troops.
It was apparent that more detailed information as to the
nature and management of functional nervous disorders
among soldiers was necessary and, so, under an appropriation made by the Rockefeller Foundation, Dr. Salmon
left in May, 1917, to secure first-hand information
in Europe.   Before his return, Dr. Bailey, then Chairman of the War Work Committee of The National
Committee for Mental Hygiene, was commissioned in
the Medical Reserve Corps and assigned to duty as
Chief of the Section of Neurology and Psychiatry in
the Office of the Surgeon General of the Army, which
Section later included Psychology, under Major Robert
M. Yerkes.   With the data which Dr. Salmon brought
back, plans were rapidly prepared for raising and equip-
ping neuro-psychiatric units.   The contacts which the
National Committee had secured with institutions and
with physicians practicing neurology and psychiatry in
the United States greatly facilitated the rapid mobiliza-

tion of several hundred trained neuro-psychiatrists and several hundred nurses and attendants. The neuro-psychiatric examination of troops commenced before that of any other specialties and the first division sent to France has had many insane, mentally defective and psycho-neurotic soldiers eliminated before their embarkation. These examinations were developed to such an extent that over 72,000 men were rejected from the draft army because of neuro-psychiatric disorders. Largely as a result of this remarkable work organized by Colonel Bailey, the rate of mental and nervous cases evacuated to the United States from France was less than that from any expeditionary force in history. The incidence of mental disease in the A. E. F. was one-third lower than the rate among the troops on the Mexican border in 1916. The total number of patients sent home for the neuroses ("shell-shock") was a little over 2,000. The rate for suicides in the A. E. F. was phenomenally low, being only one-tenth that in the Regular Army in 1915. The elimination of mentally defective and psychopathic soldiers in the camps at home was also a factor of prime importance in the remarkably low prevalence of serious crime in the A. E. F. Of the 2,000,000 men who left this country for France only 1,700 were returned as general prisoners. Not only was there much less crime in the A. E. F. than in the relatively unselected Regular Army, but there was less than in the civil population of the same group in size and age-period.

In every medical activity of the Army at home the

problems of mental diseases received recognition. Base and general hospitals had neuro-psychiatric wards; psychiatric clinics were organized in all military prisons, in one of which a school of instruction was maintained; five civil centers were utilized for the instruction of medical officers in neuro-psychiatry; a school of instruction for psychiatric social workers was established; co-operation was secured from State officials for the reception of men discharged from the Army for mental disabilities, and laws were passed in several States authorizing their voluntary admission to hospitals.

In France, Colonel Salmon became Senior Consultant in Neuro-psychiatry to the A. E. F. and was instrumental in organizing base and advanced hospitals for the treatment of mental and nervous disorders. The special hospital for war neuroses at Lafauche, France, was the first special base hospital to operate in the A. E. F. Colonel Bailey, who was later assisted in the office of the Surgeon General by Lt. Colonel Frankwood E. Williams of the staff of the National Committee, had secured President Wilson's approval of the assignment of Division neuro-psychiatrists, the first specialists attached to Divisions, and in France the same decision was made. The result of having these highly trained officers serving with troops in combat, the provision of advanced hospitals a few miles from the firing lines for treatment of neuro-psychiatric patients, and the effects of the exclusion of thousands of potential mental patients from the draft army in the United States, resulted in the control of the prevalence of these disorders at the front to a degree which could not have been obtained in any other way. This conservation of man-power was recognized by General Pershing in a personal message of thanks, to Colonel Salmon, for what had been accomplished by the Army neuro-psychiatrists at the front.

The part played by The National Committee for Mental Hygiene in the war has been stated by Surgeon General Ireland as follows: "It (the occasion of the 11th annual meeting of the National Committee in 1920) gives me a long-looked-for opportunity publicly to express my sincere thanks and appreciation for the untiring, loyal and constructive assistance given to the Medical Department of the Army by your Committee at a time when assistance was sorely needed. At no time has any request been made of your Committee that has not been freely granted so far as it was within your power. Beyond that everything possible was anticipated in a most thoroughly patriotic and far-seeing manner. A most striking assistance was the efforts of the Committee to keep up the morale of the personnel of the Neuro-psychiatric Service. With your help we have been able to meet almost every demand placed upon this service. The files of the War Department contain many records of noble work done by your members."

RECONSTRUCTION

During the war The National Committee for Mental Hygiene had been able to make contributions which have been generally recognized as of very great importance.

Had there been no duties to be performed in connection with the returning disabled soldiers, the work of the National Committee could have been expanded at once along the new lines that were beginning to be developed toward the close of 1916. In its field, however, more than that of any other health agency, there remained serious problems of reconstruction. As has often been said, the country was as unprepared for peace as it had been for war. This was especially true in the provisions made for dealing with discharged soldiers, sailors and marines who suffered from mental and nervous diseases. A system of Governmental management, which has been universally condemned as inadequate, unscientific and administratively impossible, divided between three independent bureaus responsibility for the hospitalization, compensation and vocational training of disabled men.

In this period of confusion, The National Committee for Mental Hygiene was able to render important services. Dr. Douglas A. Thom, who, from his experience in France, was familiar with the problems of ex-service men suffering from mental and nervous diseases, was employed by the National Committee to visit large centers in all parts of the country for the purpose of gathering information that would be useful to Government officials dealing with the problem in Washington and to obtain local co-operation between the representatives of the American Red Cross, the U. S. Public Health Service, the Federal Board for Vocational Education, the Bureau of War Risk Insurance and the local civil hospitals and clinics in handling the immediate situation. Many patients benefited from this co-operation between Government and local agencies. Where facilities did not exist, special clinics were organized. Through the advice of Dr. Thom, Division psychiatrists were appointed to a number of the Administrative Divisions of the Red Cross dealing with ex-soldier relief. At the same time co-operation was further extended by the activities of Miss V. M. Macdonald, appointed by The National Committee for Mental Hygiene, for a temporary period, to assist local agencies throughout 'the country in obtaining the services of suitably trained psychiatric social workers. By means of a special fund donated by Mrs. Elizabeth Milbank Anderson, it became possible for the National Committee to supply competent psychiatric social workers, for work among mentally disabled ex-service men, to the following communities: Philadelphia, Chicago, New Haven, Newark, St. Louis, Cleveland and St. Paul. During this period of neglect of disabled ex-service men, Mr. Norman Fenton, who had been on duty in France with Base Hospital 117 (Special Hospital for War Neuroses), was employed by the National Committee to follow up the cases discharged from that hospital. Through his services over a thousand of these men were reached at home and assisted in overcoming obstacles to their rehabilitation.

In meeting the emergency described above, the National Committee realized fully that it was but temporizing with the details of a situation that was in itself fundamentally wrong. Its chief efforts, therefore, were directed toward the correction of the basic evils responsible for the inadequate organization or mal-administration that existed. The Medical Director devoted his time largely to assisting those Government officials who were dealing with the larger aspects of the problem. A special Advisory Committee, consisting of Drs. Owen Copp, Hugh T. Patrick, H. Douglas Singer, Albert M. Barrett and Thomas W. Salmon, all members or officers of the National Committee, was appointed by the Surgeon General of the Public Health Service to assist in the solution of the neuro-psychiatric problem. This committee studied the situation carefully, submitted recommendations containing a comprehensive plan for the care and treatment of mentally afflicted ex-service men and women, visited Public Health Service hospitals in various parts of the country, and made every effort to assist that Department of the Government in its work of hospitalizing sick and disabled beneficiaries of the Bureau of War Risk Insurance. This Advisory Committee resigned in July, 1920, when it became convinced that there were fundamental differences of policy between the Surgeon General of the Public Health Service and itself. The same committee was later invited to advise the Bureau of War Risk Insurance in a similar capacity. About this time the Marion National Sanatorium (formerly the National Home for Disabled Volunteer Soldiers in Indiana) was opened for the care and treatment of mental and nervous cases among ex-service men, largely through the instrumentality of the Advisory

Committee mentioned. This institution is now functioning with about 500 beds, and when the work of construction and expansion is completed, it will have a capacity of 1,000 beds. More recently The National Committee for Mental Hygiene was freely consulted in the work of reorganizing the Government Bureaus dealing with ex-service men and recently the Committee on Hospitalization of the Treasury Department, supervising the expenditure of the $18,600,000 appropriated by the Congress for hospitals for sick and disabled ex-soldiers, invited The National Committee for Mental Hygiene to co-operate with it in laying out an adequate hospital building program. Dr. Salmon spent a great deal of time in Washington assisting the National Hospitalization Committee of the American Legion in the most important work that has so far been done for the disabled ex-service men.

It may be said that had The National Committee for Mental Hygiene done no other work since its founding than that done in connection with the war and during the period of reconstruction, it would have more than justified its existence. Indeed, much of the neuro-psychiatric work of the war could not have been done at all, owing to the need for prompt action, had not this unofficial, civil agency been actively in operation when war was declared.

While carrying on its reconstruction work since the war, the National Committee has been vigorously conducting surveys of the care and treatment of the insane and feebleminded. Surveys of mental disease in two of the largest cities in the country revealed unbelievable conditions, which are now being corrected. In New Jersey, a State-wide survey of mental diseases has been made. Surveys of the care of the feebleminded have been made in Georgia, Tennessee, Mississippi, Alabama, South Carolina, Missouri, Maryland, West Virginia, Wisconsin and in Hamilton County, Ohio. These have had far-reaching results. In most instances, new laws have been enacted and appropriations totaling several millions of dollars for new institutions have been voted.

SUMMARY

The future usefulness of the National Committee is reflected in the following summary of what has been accomplished since it began work. Ten years ago there was a discouraging lack of public interest in even the humanitarian care of those ill from nervous and mental diseases. Such information as was current among the general public as to the causes of these diseases, their nature and course was largely misinformation; students were allowed to graduate from medical schools with practically no knowledge of and no interest in psychiatry; the early manifestations of these diseases were entirely unrecognized; to be cared for even in an asylum a patient must needs be "dangerously mad"; the relationship between the early manifestations of nervous and mental disorders, delinquency, dependency and general social inefficiency was scarcely even suspected by leaders in the professional groups dealing with these problems; annually, meetings were held by national bodies which discussed various social problems, but with little understanding or realization of the importance of the personal equation.

To-day asylums are becoming hospitals; names are changed—from " State Insane Asylum " to " State Hospital for Mental Diseases"; from " State Board of Insanity " to " State Commission for Mental Hygiene " (and these changes are not merely changes in name). The State of Connecticut has established a Division of Mental Hygiene in its Department of Health, and other States are planning to do so. The City of Newark has a Bureau of Mental Hygiene, and other cities will soon have such bureaus. Through changes in State laws, voluntary and temporary care, observation, emergency care and hospital facilities are being made more accessible. Out-patient departments and mental hygiene clinics are being organized and extended so that expert local facilities may be at the service of the community. Care and treatment in many hospitals has improved and the number who annually recover from mental illness increases. More attention is being focussed upon the early manifestations of mental illness; and the relationship between these early conditions and delinquency, dependency and social maladjustment generally are now recognized. With this recognition has come the establishment of psychiatric clinics in juvenile courts and the extension of these clinics to adult courts. Furthermore, similar clinics are being established in prisons and reformatories. Many States which had no special institutions for the feebleminded have established them, and soon all States will have such institutions. Organizations dealing with delinquent and dependent children, instead of planning, in a blind sort of way, for placing out children, are seeking to understand the special mental disabilities and aptitudes of children. Universities and colleges, reflecting student interest, are forming courses in mental hygiene; and normal schools are organizing courses in the mental hygiene of childhood. Collections of books and pamphlets on mental hygiene have been made and are now accessible to the public. Statistics on mental disease have been made uniform in this country and similar work is being done with reference to mental deficiency. Schools of social work are giving instruction in mental hygiene and in the two largest schools of the country a course in mental hygiene is required for graduation. A permanent Division of Mental Hygiene has been established by the National Conference of Social Work and the meetings of this division are among those which attract the largest audiences at the Conference. Social agencies dealing with various aspects of human problems have felt the need not only of workers with some knowledge of mental hygiene, but of workers with very special knowledge and, to supply these, courses for the training of psychiatric social workers have been established. Industry has become interested and special researches have been undertaken by such organizations as the New York Engineering Foundation, and a national federation for the study of industrial personnel has been organized, of which The National Committee for Mental Hygiene is a member. This interest that has permeated various fields of activity has reacted upon the medical schools and is bringing about more adequate teaching of psychiatry and the development of clinics; and, in turn, has led to a definite plan, now being put into effect, of endowing chairs of psychiatry in medical schools and providing adequate teaching facilities.

Societies for Mental Hygiene, affiliated with the National Committee, have been organized in twenty States, plans for organizing them in six other States are now under way, and groups interested in plans for organizing such societies exist in a number of other States, as indicated by the map which appears on page 331. Leading citizens in the various States, appreciating the need for organized mental hygiene work, willingly serve as members of the directorates of these societies. It is evident that in time all States will have such indispensable social agencies, or their equivalent, at work within their borders. Owing to the difficulty of securing adequate funds for the proper development of their pioneer work, some of the State Societies are not yet able to employ full-time medical directors or psychiatric social workers. But even these organizations are able to exert a helpful influence and through them persons in need of advice can usually be aided. Through those societies and committees which have been able to employ salaried workers, thousands of people, during the past few years, have been helped.

It may be said that work in prevention can never be done with full efficiency until all State Societies are adequately staffed and financed, since it is the State agency and its local committees that can best reach the individual when advice and guidance are most needed.

Work done in mental hygiene in the United States has led to similar work in other countries. An efficient national committee is at work in Canada; the equivalent of a national committee has been organized in France, under the name of "League for Mental Hygiene"; a national committee is in process of organization in South Africa; and representative groups in Great Britain, Australia, Holland, and other countries, are already making plans for organizing such agencies. An Organizing Committee, composed of representatives of several of the existing national organizations, of which Dr. Stephen P. Duggan is Temporary Chairman and Mr. Clifford W. Beers is Temporary Secretary, is engaged in the task of organizing an International Committee for Mental Hygiene. Special gifts for some of the preliminary organizing expenses have already been secured. At the back of this book, lists of the officers and members of the "national committees" will be found; also a directory of affiliated national and State organizations.

POPULAR EDUCATION

The principal reason for the slow advance in the care of the insane and the feebleminded is the amazing lack of general knowledge regarding mental diseases and

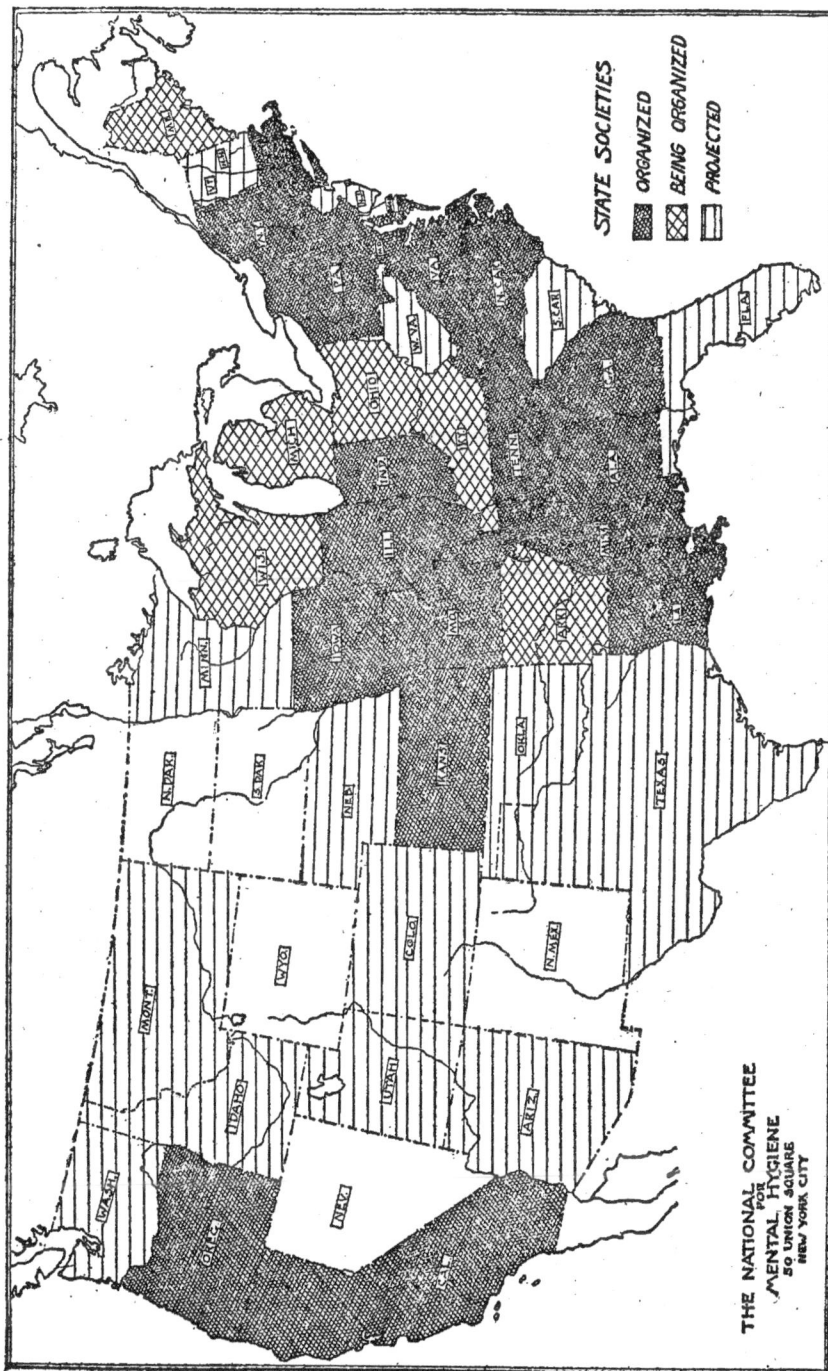

STATE SOCIETIES

ORGANIZED

BEING ORGANIZED

PROJECTED

THE NATIONAL COMMITTEE
FOR
MENTAL HYGIENE
50 UNION SQUARE
NEW YORK CITY

mental deficiency and the needs of those suffering from them. Therefore, it is an important part of the work to stimulate popular interest in the welfare of these sufferers who have been singularly neglected and thus lay the groundwork for the creation of local agencies capable of carrying on effective work for betterment.

Much has been accomplished toward this end during recent years and there is evidence of a rapidly growing interest in mental hygiene. The extension departments of several Western universities have taken up the subject and have issued pamphlets dealing with various phases of it. Some illustrations of this new interest are the inclusion of a chapter on mental hygiene in textbooks and general works, and the appearance of a number of articles on the subject in the popular magazines. The National Committee has been requested on several occasions to arrange symposiums in connection with important conferences and to outline courses of lectures on mental hygiene for use in schools, colleges and universities. A number of articles upon subjects related to mental hygiene have been referred for criticism. No efforts are spared in giving advice of this sort, for it is felt that the harm which can be done by the circulation of misleading information makes it a duty to aid in the preparation of such articles.

LIBRARY

In its educational work, a valuable library of approximately one thousand books, twelve thousand pamphlets and one hundred and fifty sets of periodicals has been established by the National Committee. It is believed that this is the largest collection of material dealing with mental hygiene that has yet been assembled. Owing to the comparative newness of the subject, most of the material is in pamphlet form. The object has been to create a library that will be of use not only to physicians, but to laymen, especially to social workers. Hundreds of people have availed themselves of the privileges of the library. A useful service has consisted in the preparation of bibliographies on various phases of mental hygiene, in response to specific requests for such information. Miss M. Florence Wilson, now Librarian of the League of Nations, was the first librarian. Miss Mabel W. Brown, who succeeded her in 1916, served until 1920, the period of greatest growth.

The development of the library has been hampered through lack of funds for the purchase of new books. Several hundred have been listed for purchase when funds are available. The largest single acquisition of books came through a bequest from the late Dr. Morris Karpas, who died in France while in the Neuro-psychiatric Service of the A. E. F. In May, 1921, when the National Committee established new offices in the Penn Terminal Building (New York), in co-operation with a number of other national health agencies, its library was merged with the joint library which now serves all of the participating organizations. The mental hygiene section of it, however, remains intact and will be developed under the direction of The National Committee for Mental Hygiene, by which, of course, it is still owned.

STATISTICS

The Division of Statistics of the National Committee, with Miss E. M. Furbush in charge, has done notable work. It has assembled a vast amount of data relating to legislation affecting the insane, feebleminded and epileptic in all States. As a result, the Committee publishes from time to time " Summaries of the Laws Relating to the Care and Commitment of the Insane" and "Summaries of the Laws Relating to the Care and Commitment of the Feebleminded." There has been a wide and steady demand for these useful documents.

Realizing that uniform statistics on mental diseases were sorely needed, the National Committee, in co-operation with the American Psychiatric Society (formerly known as the American Medico-Psychological Association), has instituted a system of uniform statistics on the subject. As a result, it will soon be possible to compare the reports of the several hundred institutions in this country in which mental cases are cared for and present dependable findings. Owing to the success attained in the direction mentioned, the National Committee, in co-operation with the American Association for the Study of Feeblemindedness, has undertaken the task of introducing uniform statistics on mental deficiency. This work is progressing satisfactorily.

Each year a statistical summary of the number of insane, feebleminded and epileptic in institutions in this country is published in the quarterly magazine, *Mental Hygiene*. It is now no longer necessary to await the publication of similar statistics published by the U. S. Census Bureau, which appear at intervals of several years and then, as more intensive studies have shown, only in incomplete form.

MENTAL HYGIENE CONVENTIONS

A distinctive feature of the work of the year 1914. was the holding of the First Convention of Societies for Men al Hygiene, under the auspices of the National Committee. This convention consisted of two public meetings, held at Baltimore on Monday, May 25th, 1914. Active workers of ten Societies and Committees for Mental Hygiene took part in the afternoon session, which had been arranged for the especial purpose of enabling the active workers to learn what others engaged in similar work were doing in their respective fields. In the evening the work of the National Committee was the chief topic for discussion. The Second Convention of Societies for Mental Hygiene was held at New Orleans in April, 1916. The Third Convention was held at New York in February, 1920. An increased number of State societies and two National Committees, representing this country and Canada, participated. When the projected International Committee for Mental Hygiene shall have been founded, an International Congress on Mental Hygiene will be held. Plans for such a Congress are now being considered.

This extraordinary progress, in which The National Committee for Mental Hygiene has played either a direct or an indirect part, directly influences many thousands of human lives and directly diminishes a vast amount of human suffering. Ten years ago a handful of specialists were interested in these problems. To-day it is probably safe to say that there is not a leader in any profession that deals with problems of the individual but realizes, or is beginning to realize, that the mental aspects of the problem with which he deals cannot be ignored.

It seems only fair to those who had the idealism to commence this work and to carry it on in spite of very great obstacles, and to those who helped finance the work, that these achievements should be far more generally known. They afford a safe guarantee for success in the work which lies directly ahead.

MAGNITUDE OF PROBLEMS

Mental Diseases

It has been proposed to abandon the term "insanity" in medicine. If this were done, " the insane " would consist only of people with mental diseases who, in addition, suffer from some such legal disability as enforced detention in an institution or deprivation of certan civil rights. Though many mentally sick persons, unfortunately, would still be insane, the majority would not be.

Not only mental diseases among those who are not "insane" (to use this word in the sense proposed), but other disorders that are classified as mental diseases only for convenience have come into the field of psychiatry. Mental deficiency—with its enormously important radiations into poverty, delinquency and crime—lies to-day very largely within the field of psychiatry as do the psycho-neuroses, which originate, run their course and end in the home, the school, the factory and the military camp.

Very few people realize what a vast domain in medicine is actually filled by the three groups of mental disorders that have just been mentioned. At the end of the year 1919, there were in this country approximately 250,000 patients in hospitals for mental diseases, cared for during that year at a cost of approximately $50,000,000. The number of insane in institutions almost equals the total number of patients in all the general hospitals in the United States. In the Army and Navy, mental diseases have for many years occupied first or second place in discharges for disability. States that make full provision for the care of mental diseases in public institutions spend more for this purpose than they do for any other, except education. In the State of New York, in 1919, *one death in twenty-two in the whole adult population occurred in a hospital for the insane.* At the end of the year 1919, thirty-six per cent of all hospital patients cared for as beneficiaries of the Veterans' Bureau were mental or nervous cases.

No one knows how prevalent the psycho-neuroses are in the civil population. Some idea may be gained from half an hour's consideration of fifty of the men, and their wives, whom you know best, reviewing in your mind the number of instances in which there has occurred, to your personal knowledge, some kind of "nervous breakdown" or other evidence of a psycho-neurotic reaction to the vicissitudes of life. In the World War, the psycho-neuroses, as everyone now knows, constituted a major medico-military problem in the armies of our Allies. Twenty per cent of the soldiers discharged for disability from the British Army had one or another of the disorders grouped under the terms "shell shock," "neurasthenia" or the better one of "war neurosis." Our own military medical officers who were interested in the clinical aspects of chemical warfare told how the "gas neuroses" bothered them in the gas hospitals near the front. The orthopedists described the weird aura of functional symptoms that surrounded undoubtedly organic cases and served to retard recovery or to increase disability. The internists gave a name suggesting effort rather than lack of it to the functional heart disorders of the soldier, but all of them agreed upon the essentially psycho-neurotic nature of the reaction. In our army in France, the wave of war neuroses among combatant troops rose until it caused no little apprehension among line as well as medical officers and then, under a system of management based squarely upon a psycho-biological conception of the nature and genesis of functional nervous diseases, subsided until it ceased to threaten the morale of troops or to constitute a drain upon our over-taxed hospital facilities. In the camps in the United States, as Colonel Bailey has shown, these disorders played an even larger part than they did on the battlefields and in the base hospitals of France.

Mental Deficiency

It is conservatively estimated that there are in the United States at least 300,000 mentally deficient or, as they are more commonly called, feebleminded persons, of whom fewer than 50,000 are in institutions. It is believed that in the State of New York alone there are 40,000 feebleminded persons outside of institutions. All of the feebleminded do not require institutional care, but a great increase in institutional provision is urgently needed throughout the country.

Delinquency

Each year in this country alone about 500,000 men, women and children at least half of whom are mentally disordered, mentally deficient or unstable individuals, pass through the courts into correctional institutions. The hand of the law falls not only upon this great army of convicted offenders, but also upon an undetermined, but certainly very large number of quite innocent persons who suffer shame, loneliness or destitution through the sudden loss of those upon whom they are in some measure dependent. Imprisonment of wage earners ranks with desertion, tuberculosis and mental diseases as a cause of dependence among young mothers and their children. The financial cost of imprisoning 500,000 persons each year is enormous, but it represents only a part of the cost of the effort which every community must constantly put forth to repress crime.

PREVENTION

Mankind's warfare against disease has been conducted in two great phases. The first, following many centuries of entire defenselessness, consisted wholly in the erection of special defenses during emergencies. This was the period of quarantines, segregation of infected persons and the beginning of efforts to eliminate poisons from food, air and water. In the second phase, that through which we are now passing, we seek to supplement, or in some directions actually to substitute for, the defensive measures of the first phase, efforts to anticipate disease by destroying its agencies before imminent danger exists and to fortify the natural powers of human resistance through increasing immunity and bodily vigor. It is as much an object, in this phase, to enable the weak to become strong, the strong to become stronger, the healthy to become healthier and the vigorous to become more vigorous as it is to prevent disease and to defer death.

It is believed that with the knowledge now in our possession, with opportunity to make widely known the enormously important lessons in mental hygiene taught by the war and with the receptive public attitude that now exists, mental hygiene may take its place by the side of other major activities in the great field of preventive medicine. In helping to place it there, The National Committee for Mental Hygiene will simply be carrying out its chief objective: work in prevention.

CONCLUSION

In the foregoing pages, with many omissions and with many important and productive activities merely indicated, there have been outlined the steps by which a new health movement originated, grew, developed practical methods, found useful fields in which to work, served our country in a great war, and gradually won recognition and support. Never, except for the first three years, supplied with sufficient funds to undertake half the tasks that lay clearly before it, The National Committee for Mental Hygiene is to-day making its influence felt in many parts of the wide domain in which mental disorders cloud the lives of individuals and menace the security of society.

The time has come to appeal to the public to provide the support that heretofore has been given by the few. The time has come for stabilizing, upon the permanent foundation of endowment, work already under way that cannot be abandoned, for developing along new lines, disclosed by what has been accomplished, and for participating more fully in the organized health and social activities of every community. Under sound, experienced, scientific direction, with adequate financial support and the continued confidence of the great philanthropic foundations that have investigated its work and approved its methods, The National Committee for Mental Hygiene can play a very large part in the future in limiting the ravages of a group of grave diseases, increasing the fullness and efficiency of life for those who have to battle with lesser mental handicaps, promoting the salvage and profitable use of much defective human material, lifting some almost intolerable burdens from childhood, and pointing the way to more effective management of social ills in which mental factors exert a controlling influence.

III

PUBLICATIONS

A large number of pamphlets and reports, issued or distributed by The National Committee for Mental Hygiene, many of which may be had for the asking, are listed on pages following this description of its official quarterly magazine, the publication of which was begun in January, 1917.

MENTAL HYGIENE

A New Magazine in a New Field

AIM

Mental Hygiene aims to present non-technical articles on the practical management of mental problms in all relations of life.

FIELD

Adaptation of education to needs of the individual.

Study of mental factors in dependency, delinquency, crime and industry.

Management of alcoholism and drug addiction.

Control of mental deficiency.

Prevention and treatment of mental diseases and epilepsy.

FOR

All thoughtful readers—especially physicians, lawyers, clergymen, educators, public officials, and students of social problems.

Mental Hygiene will present to a wide circle of readers popular articles on the practical management of mental problems in all relations of life. These articles will give the results of study and work in new and vitally important enterprises. To-day, as never before, attention is being directed to mental factors in the problems of the individual and of society. These factors are of paramount importance in the study and practical management of delinquency, crime and inebriety. We no longer ignore the fact that education must meet the needs of children who present special difficulties of adaption. The widespread determination to control feeblemindedness raises questions of economics, law, and medicine which demand the most thoughtful consideration. New ideals in the care and treatment of those suffering from mental disorders are imposing new obligations upon the public authorities. The recognition of preventable causes of mental diseases challenges us to seek in the field of mental hygiene victories comparable to those achieved in general hygiene and sanitation.

Mental Hygiene will bring dependable information and a new inspiration to everyone whose interest or whose work brings him into contact with these problems. Writers of authority will present original communications and reviews of important books; note-worthy articles in periodicals out of convenient reach of the general public will be republished; reports of surveys, special investigations, and new methods of prevention or treatment in the broad field of mental hygiene and psychopathology will be presented and discussed in as non-technical a way as possible. Many articles that will be helpful to parents will be published. It is our aim to make *Mental Hygiene* indispensable to all thoughtful readers.

The subscription price is two dollars a year. Single copies are fifty cents each. Subscribers may make checks payable to *Mental Hygiene* or to The National Committee for Mental Hygiene, Inc., (370 Seventh Avenue, New York City). A reduced facsimile of the cover of the issue of July, 1921, appears on page 317.

PAMPHLETS AND REPORTS

It is impossible in a book to give a list of publications that will remain up-to-date. In consequence, those interested are urged to write to The National Committee for Mental Hygiene for a copy of its current List of Publications, which is issued from time to time. A few of the titles, however, are presented, so that readers may sense their nature. They show what sort of article appears in *Mental Hygiene*, as many of them are reprints from that magazine.

Principles of Mental Hygiene Applied to the Management of Children Predisposed to Nervousness. By Dr. Lewellys F. Barker.

Experiences of the Child; How They Affect Character and Behavior. By Dr. C. Macfie Campbell.

Nervous Children and Their Training. By Dr. C. Macfie Campbell.

Childhood; the Golden Period for Mental Hygiene. By Dr. William A. White.

Mental Health for Normal Children. By William H. Burnham.

Health Examination at School Entrance. By William H. Burnham.

Some Adaptive Difficulties Found in School Children. By Esther L. Richards.

A Survey of the Teaching of Mental Hygiene in the Normal Schools. By William H. Burnham.

The Right to Marry. By Dr. Adolf Meyer.

Education and Mental Hygiene. By Dr. C. Macfie Campbell.

Responsibilities of the Universities in Promoting Mental Hygiene. By Dr. C. Macfie Campbell.

Mental Hygiene and the College Student. By Dr. Frankwood E. Williams.

Mobilizing the Brains of the Nation. By Dr. Stewart Paton.

Efficiency and Inefficiency; a Problem in Medicine. By Dr. Pearce Bailey.

The Movement for a Mental Hygiene of Industry. By Dr. E. E. Southard.

Mental Hygiene in Industry. By Dr. C. Macfie Campbell.

Psychiatric Lessons from the War. By Dr. Thomas W. Salmon.

Future of Psychiatry in the Army. By Dr. Thomas W. Salmon.

Psychopathic Hospitals and Prophylaxis. By Dr. Frankwood E. Williams.

Unemployment and Personality. By Dr. Herman Adler.

Anxiety and Fear. By Dr. Frankwood E. Williams.

Relation of Alcohol and Syphilis to Mental Hygiene. By Dr. Frankwood E. Williams.

Burden of Feeblemindedness. By Dr. Walter E. Fernald.

Growth of Provision for the Feebleminded in the United States. By Dr. Walter E. Fernald.

State Program for the Care of the Feebleminded. By Dr. Walter E. Fernald.

What is Practicable in the Way of Prevention of Mental Defect. By Dr. Walter E. Fernald.

Function of Special Classes for Mentally Defective Children. By Ada M. Fitts.

State Institutions for the Feebleminded. By Dr. V. V. Anderson.

Mental Clinics in the Court. By Dr. V. V. Anderson.

A National Deficit (Mental Deficiency). By Dr. V. V. Anderson.

Education of Mental Defectives in State and Private Institutions and in Special Classes in Public

Schools in the United States. By Dr. V. V. Anderson.

Mental Deficiency; Its Frequency and Characteristics in the United States as Determined by the Examination of Recruits. By Dr. Pearce Bailey and Roy Haber.

Feeblemindedness and the Law. By Dr. Thomas W. Salmon.

Colony and Extra-Institutional Care for the Feebleminded. By Dr. Charles Bernstein.

Type of Feebleminded Who Can be Cared for in the Community. By Dr. George N. Wallace.

Types of Delinquent Careers. By Dr. Bernard Glueck.

Concerning Prisoners. By Dr. Bernard Glueck.

Medico-psychological Study of Delinquents. By Dr. William Healy and Augusta F. Bronner.

Three Cases of Larceny. By Dr. Edith R. Spaulding.

Disciplinary Measures in the Management of the Psychopathic Woman. By Jessie D. Hodder.

Community Organization for Mental Hygiene. By Dr. Owen Copp.

Barriers to the Treatment of Mental Patients. By Dr. Owen Copp.

Community Responsibility in the Treatment of Mental Disorders. By Dr. William L. Russell.

Mental Pitfalls of Adolescence. By Dr. Henry R. Stedman.

Why Should So Many Go Insane? By Homer Folks and Everett Elwood.

Psychiatric Social Work. By Mary C. Jarrett.

Social Service for the Mentally Sick a Good Investment
for the State. By V. M. Macdonald.

Purposes, Plans and Work of State Societies for
Mental Hygiene. By Clifford W. Beers.

Outline of a State Society for Mental Hygiene. By
Dr. E. Stanley Abbot.

The Possibilities of a State Society for Mental Hygiene.
By Dr. H. Douglas Singer.

Dementia Praecox as a Social Problem. By Horatio
M. Pollock.

Decline of Alcohol as a Cause of Insanity. By Horatio
M. Pollock.

Annual Census of the Insane, Feebleminded, Epileptics
and Inebriates in Institutions in the United States.
By Horatio M. Pollock and Edith M. Furbush.
Issued each year by The National Committee for
Mental Hygiene.

Statistical Manual for the use of Institutions for Mental
Diseases. By Bureau of Statistics of The National
Committee for Mental Hygiene.

Summaries of State Laws Relating to the Insane.
(Price $1.00). Issued, from time to time, by The
National Committee for Mental Hygiene.

Summaries of State Laws Relating to the Feebleminded
and Epileptic. (Price,$1.00.) Issued, from time
time, by The National Committee for Mental
Hygiene.

IV

THE NATIONAL COMMITTEE FOR MENTAL HYGIENE

370 Seventh Avenue, New York City.

(Penn Terminal Building, Corner of 31st Street)

FORM OF ORGANIZATION

Officers, Directors and Members

(As of October 1, 1921)

The National Committee for Mental Hygiene, founded on February 19th, 1909, was incorporated in 1916 under the Membership Corporations Law of the State of New York. The affairs of the organization are managed by a Board of Directors, consisting of five groups elected by the National Committee, for one, two, three, four and five years, respectively. The Board at each annual meeting elects from its own membership a President, three Vice-presidents, a Treasurer, an Executive Committee and a Finance Committee. The chief executive officer is appointed by the Board upon prior nomination by the Executive Committee; the Secretary is elected at each annual meeting of the National Committee. All special or sub-committees are appointed by the Executive Committee, to which they report.

Members may be elected by the National Committee or by the Executive Committee, as provided in the by-laws. The membership, originally limited to seventy,

350

was subsequently increased to one hundred and later to not more than two hundred. It is planned that all States shall find representation in the National Committee.

The organization is dependent for support upon voluntary contributions. Funds available for expenditure are disbursed under budgets prepared by the Executive Committee, approved later by the Executive and Finance Committee acting jointly, and finally approved by the Board of Directors. At the end of each fiscal year, which corresponds with the calendar year, all of the accounts and vouchers for the year are examined by a certified public accountant. His report is transmitted to the Treasurer and, in turn, presented to the Board of Directors for approval and incorporation in the records of the National Committee.

OFFICERS

President
DR. WALTER B. JAMES

Vice-President
CHARLES W. ELIOT
DR. BERNARD SACHS
DR. WILLIAM H. WELCH

Treasurer
OTTO T. BANNARD

Executive Committee
DR. WILLIAM L. RUSSELL,
Chairman
DR. OWEN COPP
STEPHEN P. DUGGAN
DR. WALTER E. FERNALD
MATTHEW C. FLEMING
DR. WALTER B. JAMES
DR. GEORGE H. KIRBY

Committee on Mental Deficiency
DR. WALTER E. FERNALD,
Chairman

Committee on Education
DR. C. MACFIE CAMPBELL,
Chairman

EDITH M. FURBUSH, Statistician

Dr. Edward N. Brush, Baltimore

William H. Burnham, Worcester

Nicholas Murray Butler, New York

Dr. Louis Casamajor, New York

F. Stuart Chapin, Northampton, Mass.

Dr. Edmund A. Christian, Pontiac, Mich.

Dr. George W. Crile, Cleveland

Dr. Harvey Cushing, Boston

Dr. George Donohoe, Cherokee, Iowa

Mrs. William F. Dummer, Chicago

Dr. David L. Edsall, Boston

Dr. Charles P. Emerson, Indianapolis

Dr. Haven Emerson, New York

Dr. Livingston Farrand, Ithaca

Elizabeth E. Farrell, New York

W. H. P. Faunce, Providence

Katherine S. Felton, San Francisco

John H. Finley, New York

Dr. J. M. T. Finney, Baltimore

Irving Fisher, New Haven

Raymond B. Fosdick, New York

Lee K. Frankel, New York

Dr. Charles H. Frazier, Philadelphia

Dr. C. Lincoln Furbush, Philadelphia

Francis D. Gallatin, New York

Dr. Arnold Gesell, New Haven

Dr. Bernard Glueck, New York

D. J. E. Goldthwait, Boston

Dr. S. S. Goldwater, New York

Dr. Menas S. Gregory, New York

Arthr T. Hadley, New Haven

Dr. Arthur S. Hamilton, Minneapolis

Learned Hand, New York

Mrs. E. Henry Harriman, New York

Dr. C. Floyd Haviland, Middletown, Conn.

Dr. Harley A. Haynes, Lapeer, Mich.

Dr. William Healy, Boston

Dr. Arthur P. Herring, Baltimore

Frederick C. Hicks, Cincinnati

Charles W. Hoffman, Cincinnati

Dr. L. Emmett Holt, New York

Franklin C. Hoyt, New York

Surg. Gen. M. W. Ireland, Washington

Mrs. William James, Cambridge

Mrs. Helen Hartley Jenkins, New York

Harry Pratt Judson, Chicago

Dr. Charles G. Kerley, New York

Franklin B. Kirkbride, New York

James H. Kirkland, Nashville

Dr. George M. Kline, Boston

Dr. Augustus S. Knight, Gladstone, N. J.

Julia C. Lathrop, Rockford, Ill.

Burdette G. Lewis, Trenton, N. J.

Adolph Lewisohn, New York

Ernest H. Lindley, Lawrence, Kansas

Dr. Charles S. Little, Thiells, N. Y.

Dr. William F. Lorenz, Madison, Wis.

Tracy W. McGregor, Detroit.

George P. McLean, Simsbury, Conn.

Henry N. MacCracken, Pough-keepsie, N. Y.
Dr. Carlos F. MacDonald, New York
V. Everit Macy, Scarborough, N. Y.
Richard I. Manning, Columbia, S. C.
Marcus M. Marks, New York
Maude E. Miner, New York
Dr. Henry W. Mitchell, Warren, Pa.
Dr. George A. Moleen, Denver, Col.
Mrs. William S. Monroe, Chicago
Dwight W. Morrow, Englewood, N. J.
Dr. J. Montgomery Mosher, Albany
Dr. J. M. Murdock, Polk, Pa.
J. Prentice Murphy, Philadelphia
William A. Neilson, Northampton, Mass.
Dr. Frank P. Norbury, Jacksonville, Ill.
Dr. Samuel T. Orton, Iowa City
William Church Osborn, New York
Harry V. Osborne, Newark, N. J.
Dr. Herman Ostrander, Kalamazoo, Mich.
Dr. William H. Park, New York.
Dr. Hugh T. Patrick, Chicago
Dr. Frederick Peterson, New York
Henry Phipps, New York
Gifford Pinchot, Washington
Roscoe Pound, Cambridge
Dr. M. P. Ravenel, Columbia, Mo.
Rush Rhees, Rochester, N. Y.
Florence M. Rhett, New York

Dr. Robert L. Richards, Talmage, Cal.
Dr. Austin F. Riggs, Stockbridge, Mass.
Dr. Milton J. Rosenau, Boston
Ira H. Rothgerber, Denver, Col.
Jacob Gould Schurman, Ithaca
Dr. Sidney I. Schwab, St. Louis, Mo.
Carl E. Seashore, Iowa City, Iowa
Edward W. Sheldon, New York
Dr. H. Douglas Singer, Kankakee, Ill.
Dr. Edith W. Spaulding, New York
Dr. M. Allen Starr, New York
Dr. Henry R. Stedman, Brookline, Mass.
Dr. Charles F. Stokes, New York
Dr. Frederick Tilney, New York
Howard B. Tuttle, Naugatuck, Conn.
Dr. Forrest C. Tyson, Augusta, Me.
Henry van Dyke, Princeton
Dr. Henry P. Walcott, Cambridge
Lillian D. Wald, New York
Dr. George L. Wallace, Wrentham, Mass.
Dr. William A. White, Washington
Dr. Ray Lyman Wilbur, Stanford, Cal.
Dr. Henry Smith Williams, New York
Dr. William H. Wilmer, Washington
Dr. C-E. A. Winslow, New Haven
Arthur Woods, New York
Robert A. Woods, Boston
Howell Wright, Cleveland
Dr. Edwin G. Zabriskie, New York

Members who have died during their term of office:

Elizabeth Milbank Anderson
James B. Angell
Dr. Henry B. Favill
His Eminence, James, Cardinal Gibbons
Henry L. Higginson
Dr. August Hoch
William James

Morris Loeb
Dr. William Mabon
Jacob A. Riis
Dr. Arthur C. Rogers
Dr. Elmer E. Southard
Robert W. Tayler
Dr. Walter Wyman

V

THE CANADIAN NATIONAL COMMITTEE FOR MENTAL HYGIENE

102 College Street, Toronto

The Canadian National Committee for Mental Hygiene was founded at Ottawa on April 26th, 1918. Its objects and plans are similar to those of the National Committee in the United States and important results have been achieved. Its reports and other publications may be secured by writing to the Secretary, Dr. C. M. Hincks, 102 College Street, Toronto.

Patron: His Excellency the Duke of Devonshire, Governor-General of Canada.

Patroness: Her Excellency the Duchess of Devonshire.

OFFICERS

Dr. Charles F. Martin, *President*

Vice-Presidents:

Lord Shaughnessy	Sir Robert Falconer
Sir Vincent Meredith	Sir Arthur Currie
Sir Lomer Gouin	Sir William Price

Sir George Burn, *Treasurer*

Finance Committee

David A. Dunlap, Esq., *Chairman*

Sir George Burn	John B. Holden, Esq.

George H. Ross, Esq.

Executive Officers

Dr. C. K. Clarke, Medical Director
Dr. Gordon S. Mundie, Associate Medical Director
Dr. C. M. Hincks, Associate Medical Director
and Secretary

Executive Committee

Dr. Colin K. Russel, *Chairman*

Dr. E. A. Bott	Major J. D. Pagé
Prof. J. A. Dale	Dr. C. A. Porteous
Dr. A. H. Desloges	Prof. D. G. Revell
Dr. J. Halpenny	Hon. Dr. W. F. Roberts
Dr. C. J. O. Hastings	Dr. E. W. Ryan
Dr. W. H. Hattie	Prof. Peter Sandiford
Mr. Vincent Massey	Prof. William D. Tait
President W. C. Murray	Rev. W. H. Vance

MEMBERS

(As of October 1, 1921.)

Hon. George E. Amyot, Quebec	Hon. Mr. Justice P. E. Blondin,
Dr. J. V. Anglin, St. John, N. B.	Ottawa
R. B. Angus, Montreal	Dr. Edward A. Bott, Toronto
Dr. George Anderson, Toronto	His Hon. Lieut. Governor Brett,
Hon. E. H. Armstrong, Halifax	Edmonton, Alta.
Adjutant General Ashton, Ottawa	Dr. Eliza Brison, Halifax, N. S.
Lord Atholstan, Montreal	Dr. Horace L. Brittain, Toronto
J. E. Atkinson, Toronto	Dr. M. D. Brochu, P. Q.
Adam Ballantyne, Toronto	Dr. Alan Brown, Toronto
J. N. Barss, Shawbridge, P. Q.	Dr. Peter H. Bryce, Ottawa
Dr. Gordon Bates, Toronto	W. J. Bullman, Winnipeg
W. R. Bawlf, Winnipeg	Dr. T. J. W. Burgess, Verdun, P. Q.
E. W. Beatty, Montreal	Sir George Burn, Ottawa
Dr. Gordon Bell, Winnipeg	J. F. Burstall, Quebec
General H. S. Birkett, Montreal	Dr. A. D. Campbell, Battleford,
W. M. Birks, Montreal	Sask.
Dr. A. D. Blackader, Montreal	Dr. E. P. Chagnon, Montreal

Hon. Thomas Chapais, Quebec
Dr. W. W. Chipman, Montreal
Dr. C. K. Clarke, Toronto
Lindley Crease, Esq., Victoria, B.C.
Dr. A. L. Crease, New Westminster, B. C.
Mrs. C. Crowe, Guelph
Dr. Winnifred Cullis, London, England
Sir Arthur Currie, Montreal
Rev. Dr. George B. Cutten, Wolfville, N. S.
Prof. J. A. Dale, Toronto
George J. D'Allaird, Montreal
Owen Dawson, Montreal
Rt. Rev. A. U. De Pencier, Vancouver
Dr. A. H. Desloges, Montreal
Dr. F. E. Devlin, Montreal
Mrs. Arthur Drummond, Montreal
D. A. Dunlap, Toronto
Mrs. D. A. Dunlap, Toronto
W. P. Dutton, Esq., Winnipeg
Lady Eaton, Toronto
Dr. E. M. Eberts, Montreal
Sir Robert Falconer, Toronto
Dr. J. G. Fitzgerald, Toronto
Mrs. J. G. Fitzgerald, Toronto
Sir Joseph Flavelle, Toronto
Sir Auckland Geddes, London, S.W.1 England
Sir Lomer Gouin, Quebec
Lieut. Governor Grant, Halifax
Mrs. W. L. Grant, Toronto
William Grayson, Moose Jaw, Sask.
J. J. Greene, Hamilton, Ont.
J. H. Grundy, Toronto
W. D. Gwynne, Toronto
Dr. J. Halpenny, Winnipeg

D. B. Harkness, Winnipeg
Hon. Mr. Justice Harvey, Edmonton, Alta.
Dr. C. J. O. Hastings, Toronto
Dr. W. H. Hattie, Halifax
Dr. C. M. Hincks, Toronto
Arthur Hitchcock, Moose Jaw, Sask.
His Hon. Frederick W. Howay, New Westminster, B. C.
Dr. Goldwin Howland, Toronto
Mrs. A. M. Huestis, Toronto
Miss E. Hurlbatt, Montreal
Dr. Geo. C. Kidd, Brockville, Ont.
George Kidd, Vancouver
Lady Kingsmill, Ottawa
Dean F. L. Klinck, Vancouver
Mrs. J. B. Laidlaw, Toronto
Sir Richard Lake, Regina, Sask.
P. C. Larkin, Toronto
Dr. F. E. Lawlor, Dartmouth, N. S.
Sir James Lougheed, Ottawa
Dr. M. T. MacEachern, Vancouver
Dr. J. A. Maclean, Winnipeg
Dr. Helen MacMurchy, Ottawa
Prof. R. M. MacIver, Toronto
Dr. G. W. MacNeill, Battleford, Sask.
Rev. Dr. H. P. MacPherson, Antigonish, N. S.
C. A. Macgrath, Ottawa
W. H. Malkin, Vancouver
Dr. G. H. Manchester, New Westminster, B. C.
Dr. Charles F. Martin, Montreal
Hon. W. M. Martin, Regina, Sask.
Vincent Massey, Toronto
J. M. McCarthy, Quebec
J. O. McCarthy, Toronto
Mrs. Nellie McClung, Edmonton

A. M. McDonald, Edmonton
Dr. D. McIntyre, Winnipeg
Dr. J. G. McKay, New Westminster, B. C.
Dr. R. E. McKechnie, Vancouver
Hon. J. D. McLean, Vancouver
Francis McLennan, Quebec
Mrs. J. C. McLimont, Quebec
Mrs. W. B. Meikle, Toronto
Sir Vincent Meredith, Bart., Montreal
Lady Meredith, Montreal
W. R. Miller, Montreal
F. W. Molson, Montreal
Dr. A. G. Morphy, Montreal
H. H. Morris, Vancouver
Judge H. S. Mott, Toronto
A. Moxon, Saskatoon, Sask.
Dr. Gordon S. Mundie, Montreal
Hon. Dennis Murphy, Vancouver
Judge E. F. Murphy, Edmonton
President W. E. Murray, Saskatchewan, Sask.
Sir Augustus Nanton, Winnipeg
W. F. Nickle, Kingston, Ont.
Sir Edmund Osler, Toronto
Dr. J. D. Pagé, Ottawa
A. Percy Paget, Winnipeg
Dr. C. A. Porteous, Verdun, P. Q.
Dr. E. J. Pratt, Toronto
Sir William Price, Quebec
Major A. P. Proctor, Vancouver
Dr. A. P. Proctor, Vancouver
Rev. W. M. H. Quartermaine, Renfrew
Miss Helen Reid, Montreal
Prof. R. G. Revell. Edmonton, Alta.
Hon. Dr. W. F. Roberts, St. John, N. S.

Dr. Armour Robertson, Montreal,
Bishop Roper, Ottawa
Frank W. Ross, Quebec
George H. Ross, Toronto
John T. Ross, Quebec
C. W. Rowley, Winnipeg
Dr. Colin K. Russel, Montreal
Mrs. Colin K. Russel, Montreal
Dr. E. W. Ryan, Toronto
Prof. Peter Sandiford, Toronto
Dr. M. M. Seymour, Regina, Sask.
Lord Shaughnessy, Montreal
Dr. Francis J. Shepherd, Montreal
Mrs. Adam Shortt, Ottawa
Mrs. Sidney Small, Toronto
Hon. George P. Smith, Edmonton
Mrs. Ralph Smith, Victoria
Prof. W. G. Smith, Winnipeg
Christopher Spencer, Vancouver
Dr. H. C. Steeves, New Westminster
Hon. Mr. Justice Stuart, Calgary, Alta.
Prof. W. D. Tait, Montreal
Madame Jules A. Tessier, Quebec
Mrs. Charles Thorburn, Ottawa
Hon. R. S. Thornton, Winnipeg
Dr. John L. Todd, Otawa
Dr. Thompson, Regina, Sask.
Hon. A. Turgeon, Quebec
Rev. Principal Vance, Vancouver
Bruce Walker, Winnipeg
Miss Grace T. Walker, Toronto
Dr. T. W. Walker, Saskatoon, Sask.
Mrs. H. D. Warren, Toronto
Hon. Smeaton White, Montreal
Blake Wilson, Vancouver
Dr. O. C. J. Withrow, Toronto
Dr. H. P. Wright, Montreal
Dr. Henry E. Young, Victoria

VI

THE FRENCH LEAGUE FOR MENTAL HYGIENE

99, Avenue de le Bourdannais, Paris

The French League for Mental Hygiene was founded in Paris on December 8th, 1920, at a meeting held at the Ministry of Hygiene, under the patronage of M. Breton, Minister of Hygiene.

Its objects and plans are similar to those of the national committees previously established in the United States and Canada. Though this new organization has not yet secured a salaried staff, important work has already been done. A verbatim copy of the list of officers and members, as of June, 1921, is herewith presented. The active President is Dr. Toulouse; and the Secretary is Dr. Genil-Perrin, who may be addressed at 99, Avenue de le Bourdannais, Paris.

COMITÉ DE PATRONAGE

Président: M. Léon Bourgeois, président du Sénat

MM.

Leredu, Ministre de l'Hygiène

Raymond Poincaré, Sénateur, Membre de l'Académie française

Breton, Sénateur, Membre de l'Institut, ancien Minstre de l'Hygiène

MM.

Paul Strauss, Sénateur, Membre de l'Académie de Médecine

Painlevé, Député, Membre de l'Académie des Sciences

Le Corbeiller, Président du Conseil Municipal

MM.
Gay, Président du Conseil Général
Autrand, Préfet de la Seine
Raux, Préfet de Police
Appell, Recteur de l'Université de Paris, Membre de l'Institut
Brieux, Membre de l'Académie française

MM.
François de Curel, Membre de l'Académie française
Daniel Berthelot, Membre de l'Institut et de l'Académie de Médecine

BUREAU

Présidents d'Honneur:
MM.
Justin Godart, Député, ancien Sous-secrétaire d'État du Service de Santé

Henri Rousselle, Président de la Commission d'Assistance au Conseil Général

Frédéric Brunet, ancien Député, Conseiller Municipal

Président:

Dr. Toulouse, Médecin en chef des Asiles de la Seine, Directeur du Laboratoire de Psychologie Expérimentale de l'École des Hautes-Études

Vice-Présidents:
MM.
Larnaude, doyen de la Faculté de Droit
Edmond Perrier, Membre de l'Institut, Directeur honoraire du Muséum
Georges Renard, Professeur au Collège de France

Secrétaire:
Dr. Genil-Perrin, chef de Clinique des Maladies Mentales à la Faculté de Médecine

Trésorier
J. Lahy, Chef de Travaux au Laboratoire de Psychologie Expérimentale de l'École des Hautes-Études

COMMISSIONS

Maladies générales et troubles mentaux—
Président: Dr. Klippel
*Alcoolisme—*Président: Dr. Légrain
*Enfance anormale—*Président: Dr. Roubinovitch
*Travail professionnel—*Président: M. J. Lahy
Anti-sociaux— Président: Dr. Henri Colin

*Dispensaires d'Hygiène mentale et Services ouverts—*Président: Dr. Toulouse
*Assistance publique et Législation—*Président: Dr. Marcel Briand
*Enseignement Psychiatrique—*Président: Professeur Dupré
*Organization et Propaganda—*Président: Docteur Antheaume

MEMBERS DU COMITÉ CENTRAL

Mme. Avril de Sainte-Croix, Présidente de l' "Œuvre libératrice"

MM.

Dausset, Sénateur de la Seine

Dr. Debrierre, Sénateur du Nord, Professeur à l'Université de Lille

Magny, Sénateur de la Seine, Président de la Commission de Surveillance des Asiles de la Seine

Ferdinand Buisson, Député

Justin Godart, Député, ancien Sous-Secrétaire d'État du Service de Santé

Herriot, Député, Maire de Lyon

Rameil, Député

Bokanowski, Député

Henri Rousselle, Président de la 3d Commission du Conseil Général

Chausse, Conseiller Municipal, rapporteur général du Service des Aliénés

Frédéric Brunet, Conseiller Municipal

Dr. Calmels, Conseiller Municipal

Lalou, Conseiller Municipal, Rapporteur général du budget

Henri Sellier, Conseiller Général

Dr. Navarre, ancien Député

Dr. Doizy, ancien Député, ancien Président de la Commission de l'Hygiène Publique

---

Desmars, Directeur de l'Assistance et de l'Hygiène Publiques au Ministère de l'Intérieur

Dr. Mourier, Directeur général de l'Assistance publique

Constantin, Président du Comité des Inspecteurs généraux au Ministère de l'Intérieur

Dr. Rouget, Médecin Inspecteur général, Directeur du Service de Santé du Gouvernement militaire de Paris

Lapie, Directeur de l'Enseignement primaire au Ministère de l'Instruction Publique

Lefebvre, Directeur de l'Enseignement primaire de la Seine

Honnorat, Directeur à la Préfecture de Police

Jouhannaud, Directeur des Affaires Départementales à la Préfecture de la Seine

Verley, Sous-Directeur, Chef du Service des Aliénés à la Préfecture de la Seine

Dr. Cornet, Médecin en Chef à la Préfecture de la Seine

Michel, Conseiller à la Cour d'Appel, Membre de la Commission de Surveillance des Asiles de la Seine

Reyrel, Directeur de l'Asile Sainte-Anne

Scherdlin, Procureur de la République

Rollet, Juge du Tribunal de la Seine pour enfants

Laroque, Substitut du Tribunal pour enfants

Meyer, Substitut du Tribunal de la 3d section

Dr. H. Bouquet, Rédacteur medical au *Temps*
Yvon Delbos, Rédacteur en chef de l'*Ere Nouvelle*
Jean Finot, Directeur de la *Revue Mondiale*
Latzarus, Rédacteur en chef du *Figaro*
Victor Margueritte, Président honoraire de la *Société des Gens de Lettres*

Larnaude, doyen de la Faculté de Droit
Edmond Perrier, Directeur honoraire du Muséum, membre de l'Académie des Sciences

MM.
Aulard, Professeur à la Sorbonne
Georges Renard, Professeur au Collège de France
Dr. Léon Bernard, Professeur d'hygiène à la Faculté de médecine de Paris, membre de l'Académie de Médecine
Dr. Imbert, Professeur de physique biologique à la Faculté de médecine de Montpellier
Dr. Calmette, Sous-Directeur de l'Institut Pasteur, membre de l'Académie de Médecine
Emile Fabre, Administrateur de la Comédie-Française
Dr. Georges Dumas, Professeur de psychologie expérimentale à la Sorbonne
Henri Pieron, Professeur à l'Institut de psychologie de l'Université de Paris

MM.
Lahy, Chef de travaux au Laboratoire de psychologie expérimentale de l'École des Hautes-Études
Legendre, Docteur ès Sciences

Dr. Pactet, Médecin en Chef de l'Asile de Villejuif, président de la *Société médico-psychologique*
Dr. H. Colin, Médecin en Chef de l'Asile de Villejuif, secrétaire général de la *Société Clinique de Médecine mentale*
Dr. Klippel, Président de la *Société de Psychiatrie*
Dr. Antheaume, Président honoraire de l'*Association amicale des Médecins des établissements publics d'aliénés de France*
Dr. Toulouse, Médecin en Chef de l'Asile de Villejuif, rapporteur des project de réforme de la *Société médicale des asiles de la Seine*
Dr. Dupré, Professeur de Clinique des maladies mentales à la *Faculté de médecine* de Paris, Membre de l'Académie de médecine
Dr. Chavigny, Professeur de Clinique des maladies mentales à la *Faculté de médecine* de Strasbourg
Dr. Lepine, Professeur de Clinique des maladies mentales, doyen de la *Faculté médecine* de Lyon

Dr. Raviart, Professeur de Clinique des Maladies mentales à la *Faculté de médecine* de Lille.

Dr. Seglas, Doyen des médecins aliénistes des Hôpitaux de Paris

Dr. Roubinovitch, Médecin de l'Hospice de Bicêtre

Dr. Marcel Briand, médecin en Chef de l'Asile Sainte-Anne

Dr. Vallon, Médecin en Chef de l'Asile Sainte-Anne

Dr. Legrain, Médecin en Chef de l'Asile de Villejuif

Dr. A. Marie, Médecin en Chef de l'Asile Sainte-Anne

Dr. Truelle, Médecin en Chef de l'Asile de Ville-Evrard

Dr. Capgras, Médecin en Chef de l'Asile de Maison-Blanche

Dr. Juquelier, Médecin en Chef de l'Asile de. Vaucluse

Dr. Simon, Médecin en Chef de l'Asile de Vaucluse

Dr. Arnaud, Médecin-directeur de la Maison de Santé de Vanves

Dr. Lalanne, Médecin en Chef de l'Asile de Maréville, Nancy

Dr. Tissot, Médecin en Chef de l'Asile de Caen

Dr. Genil-Perrin, Chef de Clinique à la Faculté de médecine de Paris

VII

DIRECTORY

OF

MENTAL HYGIENE ORGANIZATIONS

NATIONAL—INTERNATIONAL—STATE

United States of America

The National Committee for Mental Hygiene
370 Seventh Avenue, New York City

Dr. Thomas W. Salmon, Medical Director
Dr. Frankwood E. Williams, Associate Medical Director
Dr. V. V. Anderson, Associate Medical Director
Dr. C. J. D'Alton, Executive Assistant
Clifford W. Beers, Secretary

Canada

The Canadian National Committee for Mental Hygiene
102 College Street, Toronto, Canada

Dr. C. K. Clarke, Medical Director
Dr. Gordon S. Mundie, Associate Medical Director
Dr. C. M. Hincks, Associate Medical Director and Secretary

France

The French League for Mental Hygiene
Dr. Toulouse, President
Dr. Genil-Perrin, Secretary,
99, Avenue de la Bourdonnais, Paris, France

South Africa

National Committee for Mental Hugiene of South Africa
(In process of organization: Address, Dr. Marius Moll, Bloemfontein,
South Africa)
Cape Province Society for Mental Hygiene
Mrs. E. H. Lester, Honorary Secretary, Cape Town, S. A.

---

*Groups in Great Britain, Australia, Holland and
several other countries are interested in plans for organizing National Committees for Mental Hygiene or their
equivalent.*

---

*Organizing Committee of the projected International Committee for Mental
Hygiene*

Dr. Stephen P. Duggan, Temporary Chairman
Clifford W. Beers, Temporary Secretary
370 Seventh Avenue, New York City

STATE SOCIETIES

Alabama Society for Mental Hygiene
Dr. W. D. Partlow, Secretary, Tuscaloosa, Alabama.
California Society for Mental Hygiene
Miss Julia George, Secretary, 1136 Eddy Street, San Francisco, Cal.
Connecticut Society for Mental Hygiene
39 Church Street, New Haven, Conn. Dr. Wm. B. Terhune, Medical
Director
Mrs. Helen M. Ireland, Secretary
District of Columbia Society for Mental Hygiene
(In process of organization. Dr. D. Percy Hickling, Secretary, 1305
Rhode Island Avenue, Washington, D. C.)
Georgia Society for Mental Hygiene
Dr. N. M. Owensby, Secretary, Peters Building, Atlanta, Ga.
Illinois Society for Mental Hygiene
5 North Wabash Avenue, Chicago, Ill.
Dr. Ralph P. Truitt, Medical Director

Indiana Society for Mental Hygiene
Paul L. Kirby, Secretary, 88 Baldwin Block, Indianapolis
Iowa Society for Mental Hygiene
(Not yet active. Address: National Committee, 370 Seventh Avenue, New York)
Kansas Society for Mental Hygiene
Dr. Florence B. Sherbon, Secretary, Mulvane Building, Topeka, Kans.
Kentucky Society for Mental Hygiene
(In process of organization. Address: National Committee)
Louisiana Society for Mental Hygiene
Dr. Maud Loeber, Secretary, 4124 Milan Street, New Orleans, La.
Maine Society for Mental Hygiene
(In process of organization. Address: Dr. F. C. Tyson, Augusta, Me.)
Maryland Society for Mental Hygiene
130 So. Calvert Street, Baltimore, Md. Dr. Chas. B. Thompson, Exec. Secretary
Massachusetts Society for Mental Hygiene
1132 Kimball Building, 18 Tremont Street, Boston, Mass.
Dr. A. Warren Stearns, Exec. Secretary
Michigan Society for Mental Hygiene
(In process of organization. Address: National Committee)
Mississippi Society for Mental Hygiene
Dr. J. H. Fox, Secretary, Jackson, Miss.
Missouri Society for Mental Hygiene
Dr. James F. McFadden, Secretary, Humboldt Building, St. Louis, Mo.
(New York) Mental Hygiene Committee of the State Charities Aid Association
105 East 22d Street, New York City, George A. Hastings, Exec. Secretary
Mrs. Margaret J. Powers, Social Service Director
North Carolina Society for Mental Hygiene
Dr. Albert Anderson, Secretary, Raleigh, N. C.
Ohio Society for Mental Hygiene
(In process of organization. Address: National Committee)
Oregon Society for Mental Hygiene
Professor Samual C. Kohs, Secretary, Portland, Ore.
(Penna.) Mental Hygiene Committee of the Public Charities Association,
419 South 15th Street, Philadelphia, Pa., Dr. E. Stanley Abbot, Medical Director

Norbert J. Melville, Associate in Psychology

Kenneth L. M. Pray, Secretary

Rhode Island Society for Mental Hygiene

    Dr. Frederick J. Farnell, Secretary, 335 Angell Street, Providence, R. I.

Tennessee Society for Mental Hygiene

    C. C. Menzler, Secretary, Nashville, Tenn.

Virginia Society for Mental Hygiene

    Dr. William F. Drewry, Petersburg, Va.

Wisconsin Society for Mental Hygiene

    (In process of organization. Address: Dr. William F. Lorenz, Madison, Wis.)